Carnival Texts

To Martin Harvey – who brought my best work to life

Carnival Texts

Three plays for ensemble performance

James MacDonald

intellect Bristol, UK / Chicago, USA

First published in the UK in 2011 by
Intellect, The Mill, Parnall Road, Fishponds, Bristol, BS16 3JG, UK

First published in the USA in 2011 by
Intellect, The University of Chicago Press, 1427 E. 60th Street,
Chicago, IL 60637, USA

Series: Playtext Series
Series Editor: Roberta Mock

A catalogue record for this book is available from the
British Library.

Cover designer: Holly Rose
Copy-editor: Macmillan
Typesetting: Mac Style, Beverley, E. Yorkshire

ISBN 978-1-84150-416-2

Printed and bound by Gutenberg Press, Malta.

Contents

Contents

Preface

Carnival Texts takes its eponymous lead from the work of the Soviet critic Mikhail Bakhtin (1895–1975), specifically his theory of Carnival. This is very much a contemporary appropriation, but then Bakhtin himself carries forward a concept rooted in medieval culture in applying it to such diverse authors as Rabelais, Shakespeare and Dostoevsky. The intersection of various texts from different cultures and eras is the subject of the companion essays, but it may be helpful to introduce the topic here. Carnival, in the Bakhtinian sense, has essentially to do with spectacle, and it seems altogether fitting that it should occupy a place in current performance theory. These performance texts began life, in fact, as part of an undergraduate module in Interpretive Acting at the University of Exeter's drama department, and Bakhtin already formed part of the curriculum. A more formal inquiry into Carnival seemed a natural progression from what the students were studying by way of Stanislavsky and Brecht and what came to be known as Political Theatre and Ensemble Acting. Broadly speaking, this has involved a larger than average group of performers presenting a scripted piece whose theme partook of contemporary issues and whose style involved addressing the audience directly.

One of the basic tenets of Bakhtin's Carnivalesque is the slippery relationship between spectator and spectacle, and this was key to our productions as well by treating the audience as an additional character through the removal of the fourth wall. Carnival also posits a reversal in the established order by having the disenfranchised celebrated as aristocracy. Our latter day appropriation rendered this as a celebration of physical deformity and ethnic diversity in the free play of characters who are laws unto themselves. It was not so much a case of offending the audience as of disorientating them with unfamiliar characters who behave in ways that even miscreant nationals are unaccustomed to doing.

In the introduction to *Russia, Freaks and Foreigners* – my earlier volume of performance texts for Intellect – I speak of writing about non-British characters in foreign contexts, a number of whom are also severely deformed. This present volume develops these elements by presenting non-British characters in a British setting and several British characters who are severely deformed. The idea is to create a world of the Carnivalesque in which the unfamiliar is featured as standard. This may well be interpreted by some as postmodern and as a dystopia, and they are welcome to their views. My own view, for all that it is worth, is that this special meaning of Carnival empowers both spectator and performer and celebrates what in more familiar contexts would be shunned as grotesque to the point of repulsive. Our aim was not so much to suspend judgement as to invite engagement with the unfamiliar through Carnivalesque celebration and, if possible, laughter.

In the case of *Strangers To Paradise* – the signal text, performed out-of-doors, in a carnival setting – spectator response was ideally receptive. People were especially responsive to the forthright presentation of deformity, laughing in a way I had never known them to do. The aim was similar to the aim of disabled stand-up comedians like Liz Carr and Laurence Clark, who invite their audiences to laugh at the interaction between the disabled and the ordinary public – without depicting the one as saintly victims or the other as inhuman villains. The humour was simply in the juxtaposition of the strange and the less strange. Judgement might be withheld through the inability to categorize – a welcome element of all artistic expression. But certainly the spectators' predilection to laugh in the presence of physical deformity was cause for Carnivalesque celebration. This is the governing feature of all three texts, as it was of their productions.

These texts could be marketed as disability plays, since I am congenitally disabled and these partake directly of my disabled experience. But the term 'disability' suggests a relaxing of standards and a special-interest audience, and, in this sense, I would no more wish to be a 'disability' playwright than Tennessee Williams is a 'gay' playwright. He used his unique experience to comment on the general human condition; that's how I'd like to use mine. The demarcations aren't always clear, though. The incidence of discrimination and interaction with the police is very much based on personal experience. The director/ module leader encouraged me to be as open as I dared about my experience. To illustrate how this translates into dramatic action, I was once targeted by a young cerebral palsy woman for money. If the transaction had been allowed to take place, I'd have given her everything I had on me except for the fare home. But someone who knew her caught sight of us and intervened: 'Is this guy bothering you, Kate?' And he proceeded to knock me over and 'rescue' the woman. The normal response would be to tell the man I was trying to help the woman. But would an able-bodied person even have been stopped? I don't want to come across as a victim, but my point is that this is an experience that only a disabled person would know, and in these plays I'm using that uniqueness to comment on the human condition.

Chronic disability revises everything one knows about the status quo: how one receives and bestows love, the sources of income one has, literally, how one moves and interacts with the world as a whole. Some day there is going to be a movement where disabled experience takes its place alongside ethnic, gender and orientational representations of the status quo. The presence will be greater than mine, the statements will be full and clear. I'm content that I've gone as far as people in my circumstance can go right now. But I'm also aware that these people need to go farther. It's probably utopian to wish for a removal of difference. But the easiest recognition of difference *is* possible, and this is why the Carnivalesque is so attractive to me and why it is central to these plays.

The realization of the productions, like the coming to pass of this volume, was quintessentially a collaborative achievement and needs to be acknowledged as such. This was all the more vital for the death of my father, which coincided with the production of *Brides, Bombs and Boardrooms*. Withstanding their own real needs to make a success of the project, the performers embodied compassion and sensitivity to a degree that my father would have cherished. All three groups paid me the ultimate tribute of claiming ownership of the texts and giving owners' commitments to their realization. Martin Harvey, the volume's dedicatee, crowned nearly a quarter century's working together by making these the best texts we have ever brought to performance. Our colleague, Jon Primrose, managed the technical side of the performances with consummate skill and also provided the photos for this volume. Thomas Fahy and I have worked together for nearly ten years, an association whose brilliance is reflected in the excellence of the essays he organized. Tom it was, also, who alerted me to the relevance of Bakhtin's Carnival in his own inspired research. And his colleagues' excellence is more than enough to convince any interested reader that cultural discourse in the 21st century is more vibrant – and necessary – than it has ever been, conclusions certified by the continuing courage and enterprise of Intellect and its staff. Of course, I am especially indebted to Roberta Mock and to Jelena Stanovnik for their instrumental work in bringing this volume to life. Everyone here mentioned deserves my heartfelt thanks. Without any one of them, this project would not be the solid thing that it is. I consider it nothing less than the best thing I have done, and this is largely because of what these collaborators have done in bringing it to life.

James MacDonald

Part One

Texts

Claire Holdsworth (foreground), Lorna Davis, Kim Williams and Bill Wilson opening ceremony of *Strangers To Paradise*.

Amy Mellor and Lauren Parkes disrupt festivities in *Strangers To Paradise*.

Vicki Martin and Aaron Turner in private cross-cultural accord in *Strangers To Paradise*.

Strangers To Paradise

Performed by second-year Drama students of Exeter University, under the direction of Martin Harvey on 21 May 2008.

BEATA SAWICKI	Elana Byres
BRUNO BAGLIN	Mark Ruddick
PCSO SONDRA WLCZEWSKI	Katharina Rayner
JEN DURBIN	Charlotte Vowles
KIERA McCUTCHEON	Tash Lee-Dowd
LAUREN LUCKNOW	Claire Holdsworth
EVELYN PARRY	Lorna Davis
STELLA GARVEY	Kim Williams
ALBIN WACLAV	Bill Wilson
VICTORIA SPONGEON	Vicki Martin
GALINA ZHULIDEVA	Amy Mellor
STEFCIA DUBEK	Lauren Parkes
CAROLE DEITZ	Emily Summers
AMABEL RICHARDS	Zoe Gibbons
RADOST	Aaron Turner
MARILYN MUNRO	Tess Stenway
ANIELA GRABOWSKIA	Stevie Hopwood
DOROTA WOZNIAK	Tash Lee-Dowd
PAULINE LE TOUZEL	Freny Sepai Getta
GETTA DAVIDSON	Kate Stanley

Biddlescombe, mid-Devon, mid-summer day and eve

Biddlescombe, mid-Devon, mid-summer. A carnival atmosphere envelops the town centre as the mayor and local council chair, both women, prepare for a formal town-twinning ceremony. They are on a raised podium with the foreign dignitary in last-minute preparation of the PA system. Round about, very close to the audience, an assortment of local people are attempting to engage with the audience for a variety of reasons. These addresses are probably ad-libbed for the most part. But two of the people stand out. BEATA, Polish woman, offers Polish delicacies on a tray. BRUNO BAGLIN, itinerant wielding one aluminium crutch, is also trying to sell something (maybe mainly himself).

BEATA: Hallo, mister? *Kielbasa*? Best Polish sausage? Wonders with British beer. Are you strongs enough?

BRUNO: No worries. It ent The Big Issue I'm selling. Don't let this joystick frighten you off. Agile as a steeple-jack, me. I can repair every hole known to roofs, and if I fall off, you're all the way in the clear. I got state-of-the-art accident cover. If I break something serious, you nearly stand to collect.

Police Community Support Officer (PCSO) SONDRA WALCZEWSKI hovers in the area.

PCSO: *(Approaching BEATA)* Did you know you needed a licence to trade?

BEATA: Sorry?

PCSO: I'm Polish myself, but I can't speak a word.

BEATA: You're Polish?

PCSO: Polish extraction, yes. Walczewski, but that's not the point. You're not allowed to sell in the street [...]

BEATA: Are you also policeman?

PCSO: Yes! Now pay attention.

BEATA: I not sell! Oh, no, no, no! This man sister's husband. Forgot delivery. *(To audience member, in Polish)* What do you mean leaving the house without these? I've been on the phone for two hours already. Where's our pies? You expect us to make it in this country with loafers like you on the job? My mother always said you were no fucking good. *(She thumps him lightly)*

PCSO: You can't do that either. This is an official function. You're not supposed to do anything likely to cause a public disturbance.

BEATA: We have our shop in the town. By the clock tower.

PCSO: Yeah, I've seen it.

BEATA: We got licence, sure.

PCSO: Need a different one to trade in the street, though.

BEATA: Not selling.

PCSO: I heard you. Just […] try to keep the noise down, will you? People aren't used to it.

BEATA: You should come tonight, St John's Eve. Big, big eat and drink.

PCSO: I'm going to pretend I didn't hear that. *(Moving off)* They don't really do that here either.

Mother and daughter (JEN and KIERA) approach. KIERA, lame, hangs onto JEN'S arm. Most distinctively, though, she carries a notice, Harassment is Illegal. The PCSO is initially suspicious.

JEN: I'm not making fun of you […] I don't know what it means. The size of a sandwich board, they might think we're serving cream teas.

KIERA: *(Of someone in the audience)* It's referring to him.

JEN: Who?

KIERA: I know you think I'm a monster.

JEN: Stop it. Who are you talking to?

KIERA: They imprison for cruelty to animals.

JEN: *(To the audience)* Take no notice. My daughter believes in blood sports.

KIERA: You know I don't.

JEN: Well, I won't have you standing here, making fools of us both.

KIERA: *(At audience)* That's right – this sign means *you*.

JEN: It doesn't at all.

PCSO: Can I help you at all, my love?

KIERA: *(Impulsively)* You can keep those hands—

JEN: We're perfectly fine, officer.

PCSO: Here, let me contribute […] for Down's, is it?

KIERA: You must be—

PCSO: *(Taking her arm)* We'll get you a seat near the front. *(To the crowd)* Coming through, please. Excuse us!

Dovetailing this, the dignitaries are about to begin. LAUREN LUCKNOW, BBC reporter, says something to EVELYN PARRY, OBE.

LAUREN: Are we ready to start?

EVELYN: I think so.

STELLA: *(GARVEY, the council chair)* Where's the interpreter?

EVELYN: He speaks perfect English […] isn't that right? Sir? You don't need an interpreter, do you?

WACLAV: *(Grinning)* I am very well.

STELLA: He thinks you're asking after his health […] How do you pronounce his name?

LAUREN: Look, I'm going to start now, okay? I'm getting a lot of shouting. *(To her bosses)* Okay. *(To the public)* We've come to the town of Biddlescombe to mark a small but significant piece of local history. It was here 60 years ago that a handful of Polish refugees all from the border town of Stupsk completed the mammoth task of rebuilding the town centre – the very spot where we are standing – after German bombs had destroyed it on the night of September 4–5, 1944. Reconstruction commenced in October 1945, the workmen being housed in jerry-built housing provided by local residents. To commemorate the anniversary, a number of dignitaries including Mayor Evelyn Parry, OBE, Patron of Parry House for disabled adults, and Councillor Stella Garvey, are on hand to welcome the present mayor of Stupsk, now officially twinned with Biddlescombe. Councillor Garvey will be the first to speak.

STELLA: Mayor Waclav (I hope that's right) […] Mrs Parry.

WACLAV: *(Correcting her)* Waclav.

STELLA: […] ladies and gentlemen. It gives me tremendous pleasure to be here today while we pay tribute to the people of Stupsk and to thank them most warmly for their part in, well, our survival, really. Is it too much to say that our parents and grandparents might not have lived without the selfless intervention of the brave citizens of Stupsk.

WACLAV: Stupsk.

STELLA: […] your parents and grandparents. *(A beat)* So. In due recognition of this, I think it's only fitting that we celebrate the debt we owe to all our forebears by formally naming your city our twin and by unveiling this commemorative plaque.

Sprinkle of applause.

WACLAV: Thank you. *(Speaking Polish)* And now it's fallen to me, as my city's representative, to issue yours with a formal demand for £400,000 compensation as war reparations. Your people treated my people like scum. Thank you.

STELLA: Er, thank you. I'm sure what you said was most […] gracious. On behalf of the people of Biddlescombe, thank you. And, er, I think I have this right. *Vilami*, yes? Welcome?

WACLAV: *Vilami?*

STELLA: There is such a word, yes?

WACLAV: Yes.

STELLA: Smashing. Wonderful.

WACLAV: These people are fools.

LAUREN: *(To her producer)* Hang on a second. *(Moving towards the podium)* His speech didn't read very well.

STELLA: Well, what do you want me to do about it?

EVELYN: We should have had an interpreter.

STELLA: Don't tell me. I have to have lunch with the man. *(To WACLAV)* I'm terribly sorry. I assumed you'd be speaking in English, you see.

EVELYN: There should have been an interpreter.

WACLAV: You must pay.

STELLA: Yes, of course, we're all going to lunch. *(Exaggerated)* To the hotel. Over there?

LAUREN: Is there a problem?

EVELYN: You wouldn't know what he's saying, would you?

LAUREN: Polish? If I'd known, I could have brought someone.

STELLA: Someone was booked.

WACLAV: *(In Polish)* What are you all cackling about? *(Distinctly, in English)* You must pay.

LAUREN: Pay for what?

STELLA: I've already told him the lunch is free.

WACLAV: Four hundred zero, zero, zero.

STELLA: That's right, zero, nothing.

WACLAV: You must.

STELLA: We are!

LAUREN: Hang on a second. *(To WACLAV)* Four hundred for what? Pay for what?

WACLAV: War!

STELLA: The war's over. That's what we're celebrating. Today.

LAUREN: That's not what he's saying at all.

STELLA: It's got to be. Why is he here? *(She turns to EVELYN)*

LAUREN: *(To WACLAV)* You're not talking about compensation, are you? From the war?

WACLAV: Stupsk people prison war.

LAUREN: Prisoners of war?

WACLAV: *Dzenkuije. (To STELLA)* You treat us like slaves.

STELLA: But why is he angry at me?

EVELYN: You represent his forebears.

LAUREN: This is much bigger than I thought. *(Talking to her HQ)* Hallo, Brian? The story's much bigger than we thought. He's making an official protest. Hallo? Hallo!

STELLA: No, he's not. What are you putting about? This is a celebration. Stop filming! I order you.

LAUREN: What, government censorship? Hallo!

STELLA: Are you out of your mind? It's an international incident!

EVELYN: *(To LAUREN)* Can't you see you're not helping?

LAUREN: We've already stopped. But that's not the point. This is about public interest […] the people's right to know. *(To base)* Can anybody find Brian Moyles?

EVELYN: *(To STELLA)* Look. Why don't you move him in that general direction, and I'll do whatever I can to find the interpreter. I'm sure one was organized.

WACLAV: What happen? We now eat?

STELLA: What? Yes, of course! We're going there right now. The Devonian. Just over there. I was sure that's all you were saying.

WACLAV: But you pay.

STELLA: Yes, of course. We pay for everything.

WACLAV: Everything! Good!

They go off, perhaps with WACLAV leading her with an arm round her shoulder. Overlapping, BAGLIN continues his harangue at the audience.

BRUNO: *(Looking away from the spectacle)* Did you buy a pie from her, did you? All right, I'm not pointing the finger, especially at a wench. What's the betting her old man is rat-arsed at home. And she's after your cash, isn't arsed how she gets it, and he wants our whole fucking jobs. What'd he tell Immigration? He's a builder, like me, and he charges you less, so, of course, you believe him. Refugee type, he'll work like a born slave. And the job's done in double quick time. Flash forward some evening next autumn [...] there are warnings of floods and you're thinking, Am I laughing the roof's done in time. It's a laugh that's more like a wet fart, I tell you. Your worries are only begun. You notice some damp on the ceiling, and you're thinking, Well, they said we'd be having two inches. and then, Oh, my God, it's right there. And even if you fool yourself it's only a matter of one or two slates, you're up there the next night a whole row of slates to the bad. Then your inside timbers is soggy and your best mate tells you those aren't the right nails. And then you remember the job wasn't certified anyway, and the bastard's long gone back to Catamaran by this time. Have you heard me? Could she sell you so much as a postage stamp now? And I'd love to tell you I'm sorry, but you'd hit me, and that still wouldn't get you a new roof. I'm only glad I been able to warn you.

PCSO: *(Approaching him)* Are you making yourself unpopular?

BRUNO: Me? No, I'm taking the air.

PCSO: Not all that quiet about it.

BRUNO: What d'you mean? This isn't disorderly, is it?

PCSO: Why don't you just move along, before you do something we're all going to regret.

BRUNO: For why? I ent got my hand out. I'm ent even busking. Are you going to victimize a poor cripple? In front of witnesses? Where's your holiday spirit? At least pass the time with some real criminals. Woman was raped at one of these events. And why? Because one of your colleagues was busy harassing honest geezers like me.

PCSO: *(Taking his arm)* I think I've been more than patient with you, and so have they.

VICTORIA SPUNGEON, similarly disabled, comes up behind him.

VICTORIA: I told you this wasn't the place to mouth off, didn't I?

PCSO: You should listen to your girlfriend.

VICTORIA: *(To PCSO)* A bird in the hand is definitely worth less than two in the bush […] specially if it happens to be your hand. He's sure to get shit on it, for a start. That shit more than likely has the H5N1 form of bird 'flu, which means you're for it, basically. They'll try to make you comfy and that […] get your family involved […] all the media, of course. But you're off to see the Wizard, no question.

BRUNO: What you on about, girl?

VICTORIA: Swapping you for a budgerigar. Can you find us a seat over there?

They start to move off, with BRUNO protesting, when a fight between two East Europeans erupts nearby, speaking Russian.

BRUNO: Suppose you're going to do nothing about that?

GALINA: You have to let me collect my things. They're my things. Do you want to be known as a thief? I'll tell everybody.

STEFCIA: They won't understand you. I'll tell everybody, in English, I got them from a whore for deposit. A whore using my family home for her whoring. You'll be arrested […] and then deported. Bye-bye, whore.

GALINA: We'll see who's arrested. *(Calling out)* Officer?

STEFCIA: Officer?

GALINA: Arrest this woman.

STEFCIA: Yes, arrest her. She tried to get under my husband.

GALINA: Blighted bitch.

STEFCIA: You're the bitch, darling.

GALINA: I'm not your darling.

STEFCIA: That's how I talk to whores.

GALINA: Oh, I'm sorry. I thought those were your daughters.

PCSO: Okay, okay, let's stop all this rowing, shall we? You're creating a spectacle, and that's not the done thing here.

EVELYN: Perhaps they're just lost, dear.

PCSO: Are you with them?

EVELYN: What? No, I was one of the guests – I was up there.

PCSO: They can be lost without being loud. *(To GALINA, as to a deaf person)* We […] do not […] behave like that here. It tends to frighten people. They can't understand. It could be dangerous for you.

GALINA: I don't know why she's talking like that. I can't understand a word.

EVELYN: *(Slowly)* Are you Polish?

STEFCIA: Terrible. Terrible Russia.

GALINA: Litva! I'm not Russian at all.

STEFCIA: Back of lorry she come. Terrible.

PCSO: In that case, she has to go with me.

EVELYN: How do you know she's telling the truth?

PCSO: I really think it's best if you don't interfere. They were too loud, now I'm telling them to stop.

EVELYN: You don't recognize me, do you. *(To GALINA)* You have your passport, don't you? Passport?

GALINA: *(Gesticulating wildly)* She took it off me!

STEFCIA: She is liar.

EVELYN: Have you got it? *(To PCSO)* My name is Evelyn Parry. I'm one of the guests at this ceremony. Whatever noise they were making, there's obviously something very much amiss going on. It's up to us to sort it out quickly, and, as you say, quietly. *(To STEFCIA)* Her passport, please.

STEFCIA defiantly throws it on the ground.

PCSO: None of that now. I can take you in and hold you just as well. Failing to respond to police questioning.

STEFCIA: I do nothing wrong.

EVELYN: *(After examining passport)* It's exactly what she said. She's Lithuanian. That's an EU country.

PC: I'm aware of that, thank you. *(To the two women)* You still shouldn't be fighting like you were. This is a public ceremony. People get upset.

EVELYN: If you wouldn't mind? (To STEFCIA) How do you happen to know each other? Friends? Are you friends?

STEFCIA: No! No friends! I give her work. Food. Bed. No more.

PCSO: *(To EVELYN)* I can leave you in charge, can I?

Suddenly there is a disturbance in the direction of the hotel.

PCSO: What the bloody hell?

BRUNO: Somebody let off a smoke bomb.

PCSO: How do you know about it?

BRUNO: It wasn't me. Good God, d'you think I'm barking?

EVELYN: But that's where they're having lunch.

They start off.

BRUNO: It's like I was saying though, en it. *(To GALINA and STEFCIA)* What are you gawking at me for? It's all your fault.

General mayhem.

In an area near the hotel kitchen, STELLA has WACLAV shielded from the fray. Perhaps she is just thanking a member of the hotel staff for shepherding them both to this temporary haven.

STELLA: I'm truly sorry about that.

WACLAV: A bomb?

STELLA: That's right. But I honestly don't think it was that serious. Someone said it was only a smoke bomb […] mainly to frighten us, I'm sure. And when I say us, I mean everybody, not you in particular.

WACLAV: *(Grinning)* It was a bomb. *(Enjoying it)* Boom! *(Laughs)*

STELLA: Thank God, at least you're not angry. We managed to lose that BBC crone, as well […] for which I'm exceedingly pleased. Erm, I'm not just waffling. My friend said she'll be here any minute. *(Deliberately)* She speaks Polish? My friend?

WACLAV: You, Polish friend?

STELLA: No, not exact – Oh, what's the difference? Yes. Polish. That's right. She's also a solicitor! She's been to your country many times […] I think.

WACLAV: Good to have Polish friend.

STELLA: *(Mainly to herself)* That's right, you can laugh yourselves rigid with anti-English quips. *(At him)* She lives near Exeter […] and here she is now. *(Greeting CAROLE DEITZ)* You're a life-saver.

CAROLE: What's all the commotion out front? I had to have security clearance […] and then prove I knew the Chief Constable personally.

STELLA: Then you probably know more than we do.

CAROLE: A smoke bomb?

STELLA: That's what we thought […] or at least what I was told. Erm. Let me introduce you. Mayor Albin Waclav? My friend, Carole Deitz.

CAROLE: *(Speaking Russian)* I'm afraid I can only speak Russian […] and I don't speak it all that well. Would you prefer a real interpreter?

WACLAV: I speak Russian.

CAROLE: Thank God. And thank you very much indeed.

STELLA: Tell him how sorry we are about the mix-up.

CAROLE: Her Honour wishes to apologize most sincerely for any inconvenience.

STELLA: Make sure he understands about the bomb.

WACLAV: She seemed to treat it all as a joke.

CAROLE: Oh, I'm sure that's not true. *(To STELLA)* You didn't try to pass it off as a joke, did you?

STELLA: Certainly not. *He's* the one.

CAROLE: Watch it with the gestures.

STELLA: I'm serious. He was laughing. He even went, Boom!

CAROLE: Well, I don't think it really matters all that much. The main thing is—

WACLAV: I told them all, we want 400,000.

CAROLE: Wait a minute. What?

WACLAV: [...] 400,000. That's why I was sent by my city, the good people of Stupsk.

CAROLE: 400,000 people.

WACLAV: Pounds! Money! She said she'd pay.

CAROLE: *(To STELLA)* Did you offer to pay him something?

STELLA: We're paying for lunch, yes, I told him. We were just sitting down to it [...]

CAROLE: He keeps mentioning 400,000. I'm sure I've got that right.

STELLA: Then I haven't a clue what he's talking about.

WACLAV: *(Overlapping)* She owes us war reparations.

CAROLE: Not Mrs Garvey herself.

WACLAV: Her city does.

CAROLE: Hang on a minute. War reparations?

WACLAV: Our people were prisoners of war, not your guests! We built this square as a punishment.

CAROLE: Oh, my God.

STELLA: What is it?

WACLAV: You kept us interred – that's it. Buried alive.

CAROLE: The Russians did that to you!

WACLAV: No [...] English!

CAROLE: *(In English)* There's no proof of any of this.

STELLA: Proof of what? Tell me!

CAROLE: I don't know how this came about. But it seems he's here to make an official complaint.

STELLA: About what?

CAROLE: The war, apparently.

STELLA: But we *won* the war.

CAROLE: Without including Poland, he says.

STELLA: Well, he's crazy.

CAROLE: He's standing here, nevertheless, and a bomb's just been thrown in his honour.

STELLA: I can't deal with any of this. I've no authority. Tell him. Tell him he needs a government official, not a person in an honorary post. This is all just a matter of pomp, tell him.

CAROLE: Just how do I do that? I'm no diplomat.

STELLA: *(At WACLAV)* I'm sorry! All right? I'm terribly […] terribly […] It isn't my fault. Understand? I had nothing to do with whatever you're bothered about.

WACLAV: *(To CAROLE)* Why is she so upset?

CAROLE: Because you accused her of war crimes!

WACLAV: *(Easier, smiling broadly)* No, no, no. We have lunch, yes?

STELLA: We've *had* lunch. At least we were having it when—

WACLAV: Many Polish works in your city.

CAROLE: They were never prisoners! I dunno how I can get you to see.

WACLAV: *(Smiling)* We go visit workers, all right?

STELLA: Well [...]

CAROLE: I don't understand what you're doing. Are you making a protest or aren't you?

WACLAV: Of course.

CAROLE: A formal protest.

WACLAV: Britain must pay us, of course. But one look is enough to tell anyone, *she's* not responsible.

CAROLE: Good. That's what we've been trying to get you to see. You need to go somewhere higher up.

WACLAV: Your friend is a ravishing beauty.

CAROLE: Er, yes. She's married, though.

WACLAV: How could she not be?

STELLA: Why is he suddenly grinning at me?

CAROLE: I'm not sure, but I think we are in the clear. But watch how you smile back.

WACLAV: We'll go to meet Polish workers now, all right?

CAROLE: He wants you to go with him, is that all right?

STELLA: That's what I had planned. All afternoon, if he wants.

CAROLE: And he's particularly interested in Polish workers.

STELLA: I figured he would be. I know there are some at the recycling plant. But, you know, you needn't stay. Now that there isn't an incident[...]

WACLAV: *(Beaming at STELLA)* You like with me [...] together?

CAROLE: I think I'll just tag along.

The office of Imperial agency. Outside there may be signs of a local workers' strike. Inside, EVELYN PARRY is talking with agency director AMABEL RICHARDS . GALINA stands by, understanding nothing.

AMABEL: I'm going to be franker than usual, my dear. This is a case that calls for it. I'm looked on as something odd simply because I do get these women onto our books. Sometimes I'm treated almost like a madam.

EVELYN: I beg your pardon?

AMABEL: I daresay that's levelled at any woman who's a success in a traditionally male domain. And I think there's even some Polish blood somewhere in our line. That's nothing to be ashamed of. Witness this morning's event.

EVELYN: But Galina's Lithuanian Russian. She was fighting a Pole.

AMABEL: Oh, I saw you there with her. But they're from the same part of the forest, if you follow me, and they're all over here. I have not the slightest problem with people like her. Excellent workers. We can put her to work straight away, at your house.

EVELYN: My house?

AMABEL: Parry House. One of the regular women hasn't turned up for a week. Somebody told me she's not coming back.

EVELYN: What's her name?

AMABEL: Does that matter? Unless you'd rather not have her.

EVELYN: No, of course, that's my whole object.

AMABEL: [...] if you're sure she could understand.

EVELYN: That's the only thing – I'm not sure she could.

AMABEL: You decide. As I say, she's not really my problem. But there was a man here, just before you came actually. He said he wouldn't clean toilets [...] or repair roads with a drill [...] he didn't want contact with that sort, he said.

EVELYN: Which sort was that?

AMABEL: Other Europeans. He's qualified. Do you know what that means?

EVELYN: He's a graduate?

AMABEL: [...] and suited for nothing at all [...] a gap year the length of a lifetime. *(Of GALINA)* Not even a smidgeon of English?

EVELYN: Not even a bed for the night. I wanted to pay for a night at the shelter. But she started to whine like a lost pup. Polish woman who housed her before was unspeakably cruel, I'm sure of it. Slave labour on little more than prison rations.

GALINA: Not Polish, I. Litva.

EVELYN: That's right, I saw her passport. I even thought about Parry House overnight.

AMABEL: I don't think she ought to be staying there [...] if she's working. I'll ring up a friend right now. She lets out rooms in her house. She'll want a reference [...] is it all right to give her your name?

EVELYN: Of course [...] name, title, what else are they for?

AMABEL: *(To RADOST, coming on)* What, are you back again? I told you—

RADOST: *(Gesticulating wildly)*: They're trying to kill me out there.

AMABEL: I don't speak your language, I'm sorry. *(To EVELYN, whispering)* This is the man.

RADOST: Idiots!

EVELYN: Suppose he's referring to the postal workers?

AMABEL: They're still nothing to do with me. *(At RADOST)* I don't employ them, okay?

GALINA: *(In Russian)* Tomas?

RADOST: Galka? What are you doing here?

GALINA: Polish whore threw me out of her house.

RADOST: I meant here in England. Your daughter knows you're here, of course.

GALINA: No, and you're not going to tell her.

RADOST: I don't know where she is […] I promise you.

EVELYN   *(Overlapping)* It seems they know each other.

AMABEL: You don't suppose they're together?

EVELYN: I think not. She was on her own at the Polish woman's.

AMABEL: Neither speaks English anyway. *(To GALINA and RADOST)* Excuse me? Friends, you two?

RADOST: Yes […] friends.

AMABEL: You understood that very well. Let's try something else. Did you come to this country together […] from Poland?

RADOST: Friends, yes. Friends. *(To GALINA)* Friends equals friends.

GALINA: Not lovers?

RADOST: No, friends.

GALINA: Go on, tell them we're lovers.

RADOST: I don't know how.

GALINA: *(To AMABEL)* Can we sit over there for five minutes?

AMABEL: I don't get that.

GALINA: *(Motioning to seats)* Over there? Five? *(Holds up fingers)*

EVELYN: I should think she's asking to sit down.

AMABEL: Fine, okay. You mean for five minutes?

GALINA: *(Grinning)* Sank you ver mash.

AMABEL: *(Calling after her)* I'm trying to get you a room of your own […] and a job cleaning Parry House.

MARYLYN: *(Coming on)* Otherwise known as Gulag 36 … where the inmates are chained to the beds so you're forced into cleaning their shit … or else feeding it back to them.

MARYLYN MUNRO comes on with her friend VICTORIA SPUNEON. MARYLYN, as her name suggests, is self-styled glam. VICTORIA has a slight physical disability. Both are in their 20s.

AMABEL: This makes five times this month you've been Absent Without Leave.

MARYLYN: In these parts it's known as the Eros Project. *(Of AMABEL)* She hires us out as sex workers.

AMBABEL: They don't understand a word.

MARYLYN: Oh, sorry – therapists.

EVELYN: She means they're from Poland. Your theatrics are wasted.

GALINA: *(Vehemently)* No Poland […] Litva. Understand?

MARYLYN: Feel for ya. *(With gestures)* My name […] Marylyn Munro […] like the actress. Same name, different spelling, 'cause that really is my name. Which is more than she could say.

GALINA: *(Smiling blankly)* K-hello.

AMABEL: Bet she understood every word.

MARYLYN: I couldn't be less arsed. Only came to tell you Vic's decided to haul out.

EVELYN: Decided to what?

MARYLYN: Haul it, you know, heave her carcase … scarper. She don't want your pittance no longer, get it? Place full of gibbering idiots.

AMABEL: D'you think Victoria could tell us herself?

MARYLYN: Listen, slag, she's suspected your people of trying to poison them [...] for years.

VICTORIA: I never said nothing like that.

MARYLYN: We could go to the Service and get you shut down within 48 hours [...] and you we could bung up for life. It'd be that and all. They'd kill you, once word was out.

EVELYN: Is all this abuse necessary?

MARYLYN: Oh, my dear Lady Parry. You didn't know. How terribly sorry, I'm sure.

EVELYN: Victoria's stay has always been voluntary. Does she need you to plead her case?

MARYLYN: I just told you, yes. You'd both find a reason to stop her. I'm shouting, Foul.

AMABEL: Are you making an official complaint?

MARYLYN: You're saying the whole council's tied to you with knicker elastic.

VICTORIA: No! I'm not saying a thing against no one, all right? I just wanted to make a move.

EVELYN: Of course, dear.

MARYLYN: Oh, spare us your tolerant liberal, please. I told her to knick or damage something, just to make you look seriously stupid in the right quarters. 'I'm sure she never meant it, officer.' Pa-thet-ic.

EVELYN: I only meant Victoria could go where she liked.

MARYLYN: She doesn't need your fucking permission.

VICTORIA: And I'm not going to hear this from either of you, not in my name. *(To EVELYN)* I just thought I'd be on my own for a while.

MARYLYN: She's got a boyfriend.

EVELYN: Congratulations.

MARYLYN: Why? It isn't her first.

VICTORIA: Yes, it is, very nearly. But even he's not really the reason.

MARYLYN: Don't tell her.

EVELYN: I don't want to know.

VICTORIA: I just need my own space [...] and I'm perfectly able to speak for meself, okay? You promised you'd let *me* take care of it, or didn't you.

EVELYN: That's what we try to encourage. I think your friend's got an exaggerated view of our role and my personal influence over any of you. I'm happy for you, of course, for claiming your own space, as you say. I have far too many claims on my own space, as it happens, from people like them.

GALINA: *(To AMABEL, in the meantime, in Russian)* What are you going to do with us? We can't leave this country [...] we can't. I have a passport. I have a daughter in England.

RADOST: She can't understand you.

GALINA: She can understand my face. *(Seizing hold of his arm, in English)* No police!

AMABEL: I'm not going to ring the police, for God's sake. *(To RADOST)* Can you make her understand?

RADOST: You nice [...] nice madame.

AMABEL: I am trying to sort something out for your woman. She has a job [...] cleaning a hostel for the disabled [...] like Victoria here? *(Pointing)* Excuse me, dear, I'm trying to put something across. *(Back to the East Europeans)* And I'll go with you myself [...] to both places.

MARYLYN: *(Overlapping, looking out at the audience)* What d'you think you're gonna get, jobs for life? Pensions? Spastics.

EVELYN: Mrs Richards, please. *(AMABEL looks at her)*

AMABEL: Oh, no, Amabel, please. I insist. With an m, though.

EVELYN: Can't you see the poor impression we're making?

AMABEL: Well, what do you want me to do? *(More measured)* Can't you somehow get them to see it isn't always like this?

EVELYN: Surely the fewer speaking at one time, the better.

AMABEL: All right. *(To MARYLYN)* There's the door to the street if you want to misbehave.

MARYLYN: Ooh, misbehave. Is that what I'm doing? And what about *them*?

AMABEL: They're nothing to do with me.

EVELYN: And they're not creating a disturbance.

MARYLYN: Oh, aren't they just? Wheelchairs blocking the pavement […] CPs in the middle of the road. Coppers will be along any minute.

EVELYN: *(Scurrying to the door)* I assumed they were postal workers. Are there any from our house?

MARYLYN: And aren't you surprised?

EVELYN: Wh-what are they protesting about, us? *(To VICTORIA)* Are you their voice? Is that what you're doing here?

VICTORIA: I've nothing to do wiv em. I told you I came for meself.

EVELYN: What is it you really want?

MARYLYN: Don't get a brain tumour. They're protesting the closure of the Special Works factory.

EVELYN: You mean where Victoria works?

MARYLYN: Where she once worked. That's changed as well for her.

EVELYN: I don't understand.

MARYLYN: Well, you wouldn't, your back to the door.

VICTORIA: They found out they could pay less for people like them. *(Gestures towards GALINA and RADOST)*

EVELYN: That's something quite different. You're on a government contract, aren't you?

MARYLYN: So, what are they doing, sunning themselves? I told you, she found something else.

EVELYN: Oh. Good for you, dear.

MARYLYN: She doesn't believe it.

EVELYN: I do so believe it.

MARYLYN: No, but you will. Vic specializes in origami. What I mean is the LEA heard about it and asked her to teach it to their under-fives.

EVELYN: Isn't that rather difficult?

MARYLYN: You don't know what it is!

EVELYN: Is the object to make me look foolish or help your mate?

MARYLYN: […] who doesn't need it.

VICTORIA: And I'm not out to make enemies. I told you.

EVELYN: No, quite, we'll have to go for a drink. Today, though, I have my hands full.

BRUNO BAGLIN bangs against the door.

AMABEL: Oh, Good Lord!

BRUNO: My mistake, pilgrims. Some lunatic thought I'd look nice splattered against the wall. What's known as Live Art.

AMABEL: What on earth d'you think you're playing at?

BRUNO: I just told you.

AMABEL: Fine, we can sort this out now. *(Begins to dial)*

VICTORIA: Are you hurt, love?

AMABEL: *(Overlapping)* Police, please.

BRUNO: Oy, I told you it wasn't my fault.

VICTORIA: I'm not so sure it wasn't, entirely. You're your own worst enemy sometimes.

MARYLYN: Someone likes playing the dickhead.

AMABEL: And the damage to private property?

EVELYN: There isn't any, thank God.

AMABEL: Are we on the same side here? This has all the markings of a binge brawl.

EVELYN: But why escalate matters?

VICTORIA: Excuse me? He came to see me. Don't I have a say in the matter?

BRUNO: That's right, and I did some work for this lady.

AMABEL: Fifty hours, community service?

BRUNO: I did some guttering for you last year, tell her.

EVELYN: *(Uncertainly)* Yes, of course.

VICTORIA: *(The last word)* I asked him to meet me here, all right? And why would anyone want to smash a window in plain view of dozens of others?

AMABEL: If you want to take responsibility for him […]

BRUNO: For what exactly?

PCSO: *(Coming on)* Bruno Baglin?

Several groans.

AMABEL: *(Generally)* What? Am I supposed to say I don't think it was deliberate? He's raised my premium. Now what?

PCSO: I'm here because someone positively ID'ed him near the hotel entrance right before the smoke bomb went off.

BRUNO: I'm being stitched.

PCSO: I had occasion to caution you myself.

EVELYN: You and I spoke, too, remember?

PCSO: Someone positively identified him, ma'rm.

BRUNO: […] because I walk funny. It sets people off, like some dogs.

PCSO: The sooner you come along, the sooner we can clear this up.

BRUNO: *(To VICTORIA)* Do something, can't you? *(He is led away)*

VICTORIA: Please, Mrs Parry. If you're really serious about doing something.

EVELYN: We had a run-in before. She'll think I'm trying to exercise undue influence.

VICTORIA: But he's completely innocent.

EVELYN: All right, I try.

She follows out.

Partial shop floor where Polish women ANIELA, STEFCIA and BEATA are sorting through piles of refuse. They speak Polish.

ANIELA: *(Holding up a used condom)* Look at this, will you. It's disgusting.

BEATA: Keep it away from me.

STEFCIA: You ought to complain to somebody.

BEATA: Good idea. Let's stop work till they do something about it.

ANIELA: I don't think I'd go that far.

STEFCIA: You'd wait till you found something worse?

ANIELA: Of course not, but who are we going to tell?

STEFCIA: You don't know the English for it.

BEATA: Too embarrassed to show it to anybody, aren't you.

ANIELA: I showed it to you, didn't I?

BEATA: But what about a man?

STEFCIA: Afraid he'd make suggestions to you?

ANIELA: Certainly not, but if this isn't a God-fearing country anymore, perhaps they wouldn't do anything.

BEATA: So then neither do we.

STEFCIA: And then we're out of our jobs.

ANIELA: But I do think we're owed an apology. We're new at these kinds of jobs [...] and we work hard.

STEFCIA: Too hard, but they won't admit it. We're no better than foreign whores, after all. This is our stock in trade.

ANIELA: That isn't really what you think, is it.

STEFCIA: It's what I think they think, definitely.

BEATA: They should talk. Sordid thoughts and sordid deeds.

ANIELA: Oh, yes, that's certainly true. I've seen these advertised on television, for children to see and ask questions about. 'Mummy, what are they talking about?' And she tells them in glorious detail.

STEFCIA: Oh, yes. And before you know it, somebody's pregnant [...] at 12 and a half.

ANIELA: Youngest mothers in England, somebody said.

BEATA: I'm not surprised. It's even in the cartoons.

ANIELA: Almost, yes.

BEATA: I'm telling you. I was struck numb when I saw it and realized. Like you were, just now.

ANIELA: You saw a [...] on a children's cartoon.

BEATA: I promise you. This drunken fool of a father lifted his leg and broke wind.

STEFCIA: Disgusting.

ANIELA: But where was the [...] what's-his-name?

BEATA: And the kids in the cartoons just laughed. 'This is our papa – funny man.'

STEFCIA: And no doubt they all tried to imitate him.

ANIELA: But you said they had a [...] balloon on a kids' show.

BEATA: *(Laughs)* A balloon?

ANIELA: *(Pointing)* One of those things!

BEATA: What is the matter with you, dear?

STEFCIA: It's all the same thing, can't you see?

BEATA: Hey, girls. I just remembered [...] *(Takes out some food from her bag)* We can have lunch!

STEFCIA: Where did you get the white sausage?

BEATA: It was left over from this morning [...] My cousin got it from London especially so we could have it in the shop for the opening. I also had this, but the police were taking too much notice so I didn't try to flog it.

ANIELA: Polish vodka?

DOROTA comes on.

DOROTA: Are you the ones who complained about the refuse?

ANIELA: How did you know?

STEFCIA: Is this one of the Poles?

BEATA: Come and have something to eat.

DOROTA: I guess you don't want to keep your jobs very much.

STEFCIA: Sure, we like our jobs.

ANIELA: I just didn't appreciate finding […] that in the bag.

DOROTA: And you think that's your right, do you? Along with drinking on the job.

STEFCIA: Just what are you trying to do?

BEATA: And who are you exactly?

DOROTA: Section supervisor.

ANIELA: You couldn't be.

BEATA: Married to English […] aren't you?

ANIELA: I didn't drink anything.

STEFCIA: Oh, don't be pathetic.

DOROTA: I wasn't going to report you […] this once.

The women look at one another.

BEATA: What can we do for you?

DOROTA: I just thought I'd give you a sisterly warning.

BEATA: Belvedere vodka?

STEFCIA: *(Hissing her)* What do you think you're doing?

ANIELA: That doesn't mean anything.

BEATA: *(To DOROTA)* I'm inviting you to our party, tonight.

DOROTA: Looks like you're having a party right now. I'm telling you not to … if you value your jobs here.

ANIELA: Tell her about the […] the thing.

STEFCIA: Oh, for God's sake, woman – you tell her. Show some backbone for once.

BEATA: Aniela found a load of sex toys with the plastics. We think it's too much for decent women to bear. If you're still decent yourself, you'll support us. I'm asking you to the feast of St John, at my shop, tonight.

DOROTA: Sex toys? Show me just what you mean.

ANIELA: Well, not exactly […]

STEFCIA: Oh, St John's Feast […] here. *(She holds up or throws her the condom. Perhaps ANIELA lets out an involuntary scream)*

The WACLAV party approach.

WACLAV: *(In Polish)* I hope you don't mind us looking on while you work.

DOROTA: They're making a protest, sir.

WACLAV: Protest? About what?

DOROTA: Exactly what I said. *(To the women)* You have bosses who speak your own language, and you complain. In Poland you'd be arrested.

CAROLE: Perhaps I'd better explain. We're part of the delegation …

WACLAV: Didn't you hear what she said? They're in trouble.

CAROLE: But we're not involved.

WACLAV: *(To ANIELA)* What's your problem, my dear?

DOROTA: *(In Polish)* Look, I'm their superior.

WACLAV: Then perhaps someone should report *you*. These women are model workers. I was told they were getting a medal. You English don't know what real work is.

DOROTA: I'm Polish myself.

WACLAV: Then you should be ashamed.

STELLA: *(To CAROLE, overlapping)* What's going on here?

CAROLE: They're making some sort of protest to him.

STELLA: Oh, but they can't. After this morning? Get him out of here.

CAROLE: I'm trying. This way, Your Honour. We can't get involved in local disputes.

DOROTA: They reported for work drunk.

BEATA: Look what we found with the plastics! *(She tosses a dildo into the air)*

A bedsit in PAULINE LA TOUZEL'S house. She is in her 50s and, at the moment, walks with considerable discomfort. AMABEL, GALINA and RADOST are with her.

PAULINE: Let me be perfectly clear, Amabel. I don't think I can help, after all. Seeing them now […]

AMABEL: I understand, of course. But on the telephone […]

PAULINE: But you never said they were illegal.

AMABEL: But they're not.

PAULINE: Haven't you seen the adverts? Government finally got round to admitting it. Too many off the back of a lorry, and now there's chaos. And who's going to pay for it, Whitehall? Not immediately anyway. The taxpayer, that's who. And honest people like me. I'm told I could go to prison for housing them. Did you know that? My cell would be right next to hers!

AMABEL: But these ones are legal – they're EU.

PAULINE: They're not French.

AMABEL: Polish.

GALINA: Litvoi.

AMABEL: That's all right.

PAULINE: Is it? If you drop me in it, I'm not going to go down alone. And I've read all about these fake passports they use. You needn't try to get round me that way. They've turned the Home Office into a bucket shop.

AMABEL: So there's no way you'll be convinced?

PAULINE: About them? I'm afraid not. And you told me she was alone.

AMABEL: He came late. He's her partner, she says.

GALINA: Husband. He … husband. *(Gestures)*

PAULINE: Is he working, too?

AMABEL: She says he's been to uni.

PAULINE: How on earth can she say that? Serbo-Croat?

AMABEL: I don't follow […] Oh, you mean—

PAULINE: So his English is all right. *(To RADOST)* Come to live off the fat of our land? They say that Polish is our second language […] they'll be teaching it in our schools.

AMABEL: Along with Mandarin.

PAULINE: So we'll all become part of the Bling Dynasty?

AMABEL: You appear to be favouring your leg […] is something wrong?

PAULINE: You might think so. My foot. One of my paying guests liberated boiling soup on it. Blistered like beetroot. May need to have it off. And they did a bunk in the middle of the night. You blame me for having a caution or two? Their rooms were a regular sty. Kitchen had food climbing up and down the walls. And the bills that they left me with […]three or four thousand.

AMABEL: You must be joking.

PAULINE: In repairs. Have you ever had to go shopping for boilers? I'm alone here. They'll charge the earth. And I'm bound to go private with this blister of mine.

AMABEL: I never realized. I don't wonder you're wary of foreigners after all that.

PAULINE: These were British. Louts, but our own. Can you imagine what strangers would do?

AMABEL: Oh, but maybe, who knows, they'd be better?

PAULINE: They'd slit my throat, you mean.

AMABEL: (Laughing a bit) You'd have charge of their passports, they couldn't leave. And they'd keep the place tidy, of course. Galina's a cleaner at Parry House.

PAULINE: Vanessa figures we should put it on the market.

AMABEL: Sorry?

PAULINE: My daughter. Reckons we can get close to London prices for it if we let it go before the market bottoms out. All right, but where would I go? She'd have a fine time with me, I don't think, at the foot of the Brecon Beacons, where we've barely spent a quiet Christmas together in the last dozen years. Her kids are convinced nanna's dipso. I turn up like this and they'll put me under ether […] for permanently. (Of RADOST, who has crossed to the window) He's not admiring the view or my shade of wallpaper, is he?

AMABEL: Here, you get away from there now. Mrs La Touzel hasn't decided to let it to you yet.

RADOST: *(To GALINA)* Have you seen this hole in the plaster? We'll be spending our time keeping the rain out.

GALINA: I don't think she'll let us have it anyway.

PAULINE: They can have it for a hundred.

AMABEL: One hundred a […] a week?

PAULINE: They'd pay that for half this size in London.

RADOST: *(To GALINA)* Let's get out of here now.

PAULINE: Did he understand?

RADOST: Ve sank you, lady.

The front doorbell rings.

AMABEL: You're a fool to yourself, chummy. I don't know as I have too much more on offer.

RADOST: Ve want rain *outside*.

GALINA: Will you tell me what's going on? Where are we going?

PAULINE: All right, they can have it for 50. Understand?

AMABEL: Fifty? Are you sure?

PAULINE: […] and she helps with the cleaning. That is what she does, isn't it?

AMABEL: Let's see if I get this.

PAULINE: It's fairly obvious I won't be up to doing a lot in the near future. And you said they keep a clean house. Let her clean this one.

AMABEL: How much for how many hours?

PAULINE: Why should it matter if she gets what she wants? You can see they came here dead set on not paying any more. There's nothing wrong with the plaster. *(To RADOST)* Is there, Boris?

RADOST: I pay for two. How much, please?

GALINA: You're plain crazy. I won't have you paying for me.

PAULINE: I can't let it go any cheaper, tell her.

RADOST: I pay you […] look. *(He gives her a wad)*

PAULINE: *(To AMABEL)* Can you explain to them things like a rent book […] and the cleaning? There's no deal without that, tell her.

GETTA: *(Off)* Is there a Lithuanian woman here? I've come to help.

PAULINE: Up here […] second storey!

GALINA: Who is that, Getta? How did she know I was here?

GETTA: *(Approaching)* My mother's here?

PAULINE: This lady's your mother? But I don't suppose this is your father?

GETTA: What are they doing here?

AMABEL: You speak English? Fantastic. Your mother's looking to rent a room […] and we're prepared to give her a cleaning job. And she says this man is her husband, is that right?

GETTA: Close enough. But what is all this about a cleaning job? You mean she told you she wanted to stay?

GALINA: *(In Russian)* Just what are you telling him, Getta?

GETTA: *(In English)* What did she tell you?

AMABEL: Next to nothing, in fact. Evelyn Parry approached me about her.

GETTA: Who?

AMABEL: Local dignitary. She stopped your mother from being attacked this morning. But I don't think it was all that serious.

GETTA: What! As far as I knew, my mother was home safe in Vilnius. If she came here, it was only to see me. And I never really invited her.

AMABEL: That's really nothing to do with us, is it? You'll obviously want time to yourselves.

PAULINE: And I draw the line at three of you living here.

GETTA: That's not what she told you, is it?

PAULINE: I'll have the health and safety people after me.

GETTA: I already have a house, thank you.

AMABEL: And as long as you're telling her things, she has to fill in several forms if she's going to work for us. She can start work without them, but I can't employ her officially without the paperwork, and I'm not going to do it unless. We're a nationally recognized firm with a base of big-name clients. There's nothing back-door about Imperial.

PAULINE: […] and nothing back-street about this establishment. *(To GETTA)* Do you live in England?

GETTA: I'm married and settled here […] is that all right?

PAULINE: And you want your mother to do likewise, of course.

GETTA: I wasn't aware that she wanted to.

PAULINE: When you find out, perhaps you'll tip us the wink?

AMABEL: I think now would be a good time to leave them in peace.

PAULINE: *(Calling back)* We can firm up our plans to emigrate!

She leaves with AMABEL.

GALINA: *(After a moment, in Russian)* How did you find us?

GETTA: How could you even conceive of coming here? *(To RADOST)* And how could you let her? I pay all your bills, don't I? Last month I remodelled your house. Grandma's op has been done and paid for.

GALINA: I get lonely.

GETTA: Buy a parakeet!

RADOST: It's more than just that.

GETTA: My heart bleeds!

GALINA: I lost my job at the T.V. factory […] Seventeen years of making screens.

GETTA: I'll pay your pension and give you a holiday. Go to Egypt […] the Black Sea.

GALINA: I wanted to see you.

GETTA: You came here to stay. You're about to move into a flat, for God's sake.

RADOST: It's bad now for Russians in Litva. That's why they kicked her out. They'll vandalize her house next.

GETTA: So move the whole family to Russia. I'll pay. Only don't come here. There's no work for you here without English. Everything's digital now.

GALINA: What are you talking about?

GETTA: Exactly. You haven't a clue.

GALINA: I've got a job. I start tonight.

GETTA: You can't fill in forms without help. That's how it will be from now on. You'll be round to my house every night.

RADOST: You're very cruel to your mother, Getta.

GETTA: Shut up. Does this concern you? *(To GALINA)* He followed you here, right? And who's next? Grandma? My various schoolmates? Did their mothers ask after me? 'Can Getta find a man for my Tanya?'

GALINA: *(Near tears)* But you got one.

GETTA: Oh, yes. Do you want to know how?

GALINA: Through the Internet.

GETTA: I had to agree first to never speak Russian at home. Then given a six-month limit to find work, equivalent to what I did at home. Ian's conditions were like the Home Office. A job in an English bank or I could start packing my bags. He made it blatantly obvious I wasn't needed. I always knew better than to ask about visits home.

GALINA: I'll never meet him, I promise.

GETTA: You never want to.

GALINA: I don't even know where you live.

GETTA: If you did, you'd be tempted to turn up. Oh, he wouldn't fume on the spot. He'd just be terribly English, which is what? There's no word for it, no way of recognizing it. It's just a blank wall. But if you started to talk about Grandma at all, the cracks would begin to appear. She's coming here to be treated, of course. It's the best treatment in the world. That's after all why I married him, isn't it. I'm no better than a—

GALINA: No! You're highly qualified.

GETTA: Qualified at what?

RADOST: And we're in Europe now.

GETTA: Ian's a qualified plumber.

GALINA: What's that?

GETTA: Three times more than me anyway. Our house has three bedrooms […] and we have a car, time share in a villa in Spain.

GALINA: What?

GETTA: A house for the summer […]in Spain!

GALINA: Ridiculous.

GETTA: *You're* ridiculous if you don't think so.

RADOST: Don't talk to your mother—

GALINA: He's a banker. He wants you to work in a bank.

GETTA: He wants the bank to underwrite his company.

GALINA: So he's really a businessman.

GETTA: Plumbing business, yeah.

GALINA: So Radost, too, could be a plumber businessman. He has a degree.

GETTA: Radost has a drink too many […] and no knowledge of English. Ian's idea is to expand into the new Europe […] which means he'd employ people like Radost […] at home.

GALINA: You're saying you want me to go home.

GETTA: I don't know why you came.

GALINA: All right, I'll go.

RADOST: No […] it isn't all right. We're staying. We have jobs. And I have enough to support us for now. You know where we live. When you want, you'll come visit us, like now. Galina doesn't want you to know certain things. That's all right.

GETTA: What things?

GALINA: Nothing you don't know.

GETTA: You got him to talk. Now I ask you, what things?

GALINA: Nothing, darling, you go away. Like we are […]

RADOST: Your mother spent two weeks with a woman who starved and beat her.

GETTA: But why?

GALINA: Never happened. He's hallucinating. *(To RADOST)* Shut up […] We're going home.

GETTA: *(Kissing her)* I'll send you the money, like always. *(Opening the door)* It's really better like this, believe me.

She leaves.

STELLA, WACLAV and CAROLE are making their way down the street. CAROLE and WACLAV speak Russian.

CAROLE: Not that I'd dream of telling you your business […]

WACLAV: What is your business, please?

CAROLE: No, that's not what I'm saying […] I'm a lawyer […] I specialize in immigration.

WACLAV: Human rights lawyer!

CAROLE: That sort of thing, yes.

WACLAV: You can take on my case.

CAROLE: No! Absolutely […] I'm not that sort of a lawyer, for a start.

WACLAV: Your friend said you wanted to help.

CAROLE: With translation, yes. But I wouldn't even know who to advise you to see.

WACLAV: But you support human rights […]

CAROLE: You want to find someone in Stasbourg. Commission for Human Rights. War crimes tribunal. Someone who never liked Churchill. They're the people to see. Everyone here thinks the war was just fine […] our finest hour, in a sense. Witness what happened this morning. You want to shatter illusions. Very difficult business. They'll fight you on the beaches.

They are now approaching JEN'S and KIERA'S front garden.

STELLA: Just what are you telling him?

CAROLE: We're just discussing Churchill, as it happens.

WACLAV: I'm sure my uncle lived in this street.

CAROLE: Will you stick to one thing at a time?

JEN: Of course, I'm a stupid old woman. Someone stops me in the street, I don't think, He's going to attack me.

KIERA: That's 'cause your legs is okay.

JEN: Mostly I reckon people are kind, in this village anyway. Folk is always telling me how sorry they are. 'We're so sorry, my dear.'

KIERA: Sorry for what?

JEN: You've been at that for ever so long.

KIERA: What are they sorry for you for? *I'm* the one with the foot.

JEN: Hush now, there's people approaching.

WACLAV, STELLA and CAROLE in a residential area of the town.

WACLAV: It's here […] I know […] this is the street.

STELLA: Did you tell him we don't do that kind of thing in this country?

CAROLE: Well? Do you want to risk showing him workers drilling holes in the street? He'll say that we owe half a million.

WACLAV: *(In English)* Good evening.

This is addressed to two women (mother and daughter) busy in their garden. JEN, mother, is roughly WACLAV'S age. KIERA, up closer, is revealed as having a club foot. Both are involved in flower maintenance.

CAROLE: Just a minute there, Mr—

WACLAV: Bote […] bote […] *(To CAROLE)* How do you say it?

CAROLE: Beautiful. But I don't think they want to be dis—

KIERA: They're not – they're infected with black spot.

CAROLE: *(Automatically)* Oh, really? *(Thinks about it)* Oh, dear.

KIERA: You see, Mum? Almost all the leaves are gone from this one.

JEN: Oh, no! Oh, how did that happen?

STELLA: What are you treating them with?

JEN: It must have been all that rain we had in April.

KIERA: Can we do something for you?

CAROLE: No, really, we were just passing.

WACLAV: Ask them now.

CAROLE: No, you can't.

WACLAV: Why not?

CAROLE: It isn't polite, for one thing.

STELLA: *(Overlapping)* If you treat them with baking soda, it helps […] if you're not using fungicides.

JEN: You already did that, didn't you, love?

KIERA: *(To STELLA)* You don't want to buy us out, do you?

STELLA: Buy you out? Certainly not.

KIERA: We caught our MP snooping through the shrubs once, remember, Mum? He said he was thinking to buy. Saw you on the platform this morning, that's all.

STELLA: Oh. Well, I can assure you we're not here for anything like that.

KIERA: You mean you're just seeing the sights.

STELLA: That's right.

CAROLE: *(Overlapping)* Not exactly.

KIERA: Which is it? *(A beat)* They're here with another offer.

STELLA: We are not. I've been troubled myself with blackspot.

KIERA: Troubled yourself – interesting. It hardly shows.

JEN: Quit it, Kiera. *(To others)* She's always trying to wind people up.

WACLAV: *(Trying hard)* Lovely […]flowers. *(To CAROLE)* Yes?

CAROLE: Well done, yes.

KIERA: They would be if it wasn't for this. Which came from your part of the world, I think. Hope it hasn't spread.

JEN: It came from the garden centre in Bickley.

KIERA: Who got it from Eastern Europe. They boasted, Straight from the Valley of Roses, Kazanlak.

CAROLE: Well, his honour comes from Stupsk, in Poland.

KIERA: Same difference, ennit.

JEN: Now there's no call to take your misfortune out on everyone else.

KIERA: You're referring, I guess, to the blackspot.

JEN: Yes, of course.

Embarrassed pause.

WACLAV: *(To KIERA)* How […] your leg?

CAROLE: No, I'm sorry, that's going too far. *(To WACLAV)* I'll escort you back to your hotel.

WACLAV: We haven't yet asked them my question.

CAROLE: And we're not going to. You don't ask people like that in England.

WACLAV: No, you put them in camps.

STELLA: What are you talking about? Whatever it is, it's very rude to speak another language in front of people. *(To JEN and KIERA)* I'm not surprised you were annoyed at the fool's behaviour. The Member of Parliament.

JEN: He was crouched down, looking through our window, like a peeping Tom!

STELLA: Incredible. Well, I think you'll agree we're very different [...] Not after your vote, for a start!

WACLAV: *(Grinning, to JEN)* My family [...] live here. Family. Here.

JEN: What!

KIERA: They're after our house, after all.

CAROLE: Now I have to explain.

KIERA: You don't have to do nothing but get out of here.

CAROLE: Mr Waclav's convinced a member of his family was billeted here during the war.

KIERA: Yeah [...] so?

CAROLE: Yes, well, I know it sounds nonsensical. But we'd avoid a minor incident by saying he was.

KIERA: So say it. What's it to do with us?

JEN: We only moved here in 1975 [...]

STELLA: Yes, of course. It is proper nonsense.

KIERA: Gordon Bennett could have lived here before.

STELLA: Gordon Brown?

KIERA: No, I said—

STELLA: No, I see. Gordon Bennett.

JEN: What's he doing now?

WACLAV shows her a photo.

CAROLE: This is the man, I suppose. *(To WACLAV)* Is that right?

WACLAV: This is my uncle.

JEN: And this is meant to be the house [...] .You can certainly see a resemblance [...] See, Kiera?

KIERA: *(Looking)* What, and that's supposed to be this poplar?

JEN: It's definitely a poplar.

KIERA: But how do we know it's this house?

JEN: No, it's obviously the house as well. He came right to it, why? Imagine that. What was your uncle's name?

CAROLE: I'm not sure. Paul [...]something.

WACLAV: *(Deliberately)* Pawel [...] .Durbinski.

JEN: And he lived here in 194 [...]

CAROLE: 1946, apparently.

STELLA: And if we can somehow verify it, perhaps his nephew will withdraw a ridiculous claim for war crimes against the Polish people!

KIERA: Well, why should we help him withdraw it [...] if it's ridiculous. Just tell him he's ridicu—

JEN: My maiden name was Durbin.

KIERA: What!

CAROLE: You're not serious!

KIERA: No, she isn't. She's talking complete kak. Her name was Smith.

JEN: My mother's name was Durbin [...] before she married Lionel Smith. *(To KIERA)* Its true, love.

KIERA: Ooh, fantastic. I'm related to this cretin. Suppose that's how I got me foot!

Parry House, night-time. AMABEL, GALINA and RADOST are in the foyer. RADOST is fairly drunk. A toilet is situated nearby.

AMABEL: I was hoping your daughter would be along with you.

GALINA: No daughter [...] sorry.

RADOST: Her daughter's a bitch.

GALINA: Daughter bye-bye [...] verr sorry.

AMABEL: But I thought I made it perfectly clear. I dunno how we're going to get on otherwise. Mrs Parry told me to get you a job here, but [...]

GALINA: Mrs Parry very good.

AMABEL: Oh, yes, she's a saint. Well, first there are certain forms to fill out [...] er; you can start work without them, in the morning, in fact. But we can't let it go for more than a few days. They'd be down on me bricks and mortar [...] new Europe or not. Are you sure your daughter can't help you? If I rang her perhaps? Understand?

GALINA: Understand, understand.

AMABEL: You do? Fantastic! I was saying how we got these forms [...]

GALINA: Work job good [...] verr, verr.

AMABEL: Ah-huh. Verr, yeah. Look. *(Shows her a document)* This one's the P22, to do with insurance [...] if you get hurt?

GALINA: *(Looking)* My God. *(Heavily accented)* My good.

AMABEL: Exactly, and there are three others more or less the same […] the same for your husband if he's going to work. *(To RADOST)* You don't have that much English, do you?

RADOST: English, sure […] *(Wails off-key)* We are the champions/ We are/ We are/We are the champions of Eurovisions!

AMABEL: Yeah, all right.

RADOST: So you gotta vote, vote, vote for the champions!

AMABEL: That reminds me. Drinking is out, okay? No drink.

RADOST: Okay!

AMABEL: No, it's not okay. The way you are right now, we can't use you. You'd frighten the residents […] they're more sensitive than everybody. They'd make accusations against you […] something I couldn't afford. I'm not sure you wouldn't frighten other cleaners […] a bad job all round.

RADOST: I do good job for you. I clean good.

AMABEL: I don't think I can take the risk, sorry. Like I told you before, you're too qualified. You belong on a farm p'haps […] or a factory somewhere. I know you don't want other Poles, but, realistically speaking, what else is there.

RADOST: Polish! *(Spits)*

AMABEL: I know. I felt you the first time.

GALINA: Litvoi […] Litvoi!

AMABEL: I couldn't be more sorry. *(To GALINA)* I daren't risk it.

GALINA: *(urgently)* Plis, madam.

AMABEL: Please stop pawing me. If he'd come here sober, shown some willing. But how can you even ask, in a way?

GALINA: Sank you verr much.

AMABEL: Wait a minute. You want a job, don't you? Are you telling me you drink as well? Drink? You?

GALINA: Ah, no! Drink – Terrible. *(She makes a spitting gesture)*

AMABEL: That's what I thought. I think you'll be fine once we get through the paperwork. You want to come with me for a minute? I'll show you what you'll be doing.

GALINA follows him, trying to understand what he says by his movement. RADOST takes her lead, speaking to her from time to time.

AMABEL: You'll be working three hours a day from 6.00 to 9.00, seven pounds per hour. Mainly the foyer here and the toilets, six in all. There'll be another girl with you, but not always the same girl. We have four at the moment, and you'll be taking it in turns. For instance, tomorrow you'll be working with Marylyn, the girl you met at my place. She's not the most reliable, but I don't expect you to do her work if she doesn't turn up. If that happens, you ring my mobile, right? Don't worry you're disturbing me. I need to know if she's not here.

RADOST: Doesn't she know we can't understand a thing she says?

GALINA: Shut up, I can't hear her.

RADOST: You can't understand anyway.

AMABEL: *(Raising her voice)* I don't know why she took the job. Her family are richer than Croesus. But that shouldn't mean she can let people down. *(Pointing to the cupboard)* This is the supply cupboard. All your cleaning materials are here […] and here are the incontinence pads and things. *(Tries to look past RADOST, who moves too close to him)* […] because a number of the residents are fairly helpless. *(Side-stepping him altogether)* But you don't really need to bother about that. We have a full nursing staff for that. It's not your job.

RADOST: Talk slow. We no understand.

AMABEL: Excuse me. *(To GALINA)* You did explain that there's no job for him. I won't be intimidated.

GALINA: I told you to shut up. You want her to have you kicked me out?

RADOST: I don't like her.

GALINA: You're just jealous [...] and you're drunk. *(To AMABEL)* Sorry [...] verr sorry.

AMABEL: As long as that's understood. *(His mobile rings)* Oh, damn, who's that. *(To GALINA)* Will you excuse me a minute? *(Responding)* Hallo? Who's calling, please [...]? Well, can't you deal with it? I'm in the middle of interviewing? *(Waits)* Well, all right, I'll be right up. There's no point in having a miscarriage. *(To GALINA)* I'm really sorry about this. Someone's playing silly beggars on the top floor.

GALINA: Sorry?

AMABEL: I'll be right – as soon as I can, all right? You'll be fine. *(Going off)* Wait for me!

GALINA: Verr sorry.

RADOST: She's a fucking crook.

GALINA: Shut up [...] I told you to shut up.

RADOST: We don't need her fucking [...] toilets!

GALINA: I need them, all right? I'm fucking ignorant. I haven't got a degree [...] You ruined my chance of a job here [...] my relationship with Getta.

RADOST: Fucking bitch.

GALINA: That's right. Only my bitch of a daughter.

RADOST: We're better off.

GALINA: Better off how [...] and who with, you? Who are you?

RADOST: I'm your—

GALINA: You're a stinking Russian immigrant [...] homeless, stateless, and you pissed yourself with drink. I never asked you to come [...] I don't want to see you again, get it?

RADOST: You're just tired.

GALINA: *(Produces sharp scissors)* Are you going to leave or am I going to try for your balls? I could do it, too, with you like you are [...] and whatever I did, you'd scream like a pig.

RADOST: All right, calm down.

GALINA: Start screaming.

RADOST: I'm leaving, all right? And I'm not going to drink any more. You'll see. *(He goes off)*

GALINA stands dazed for some moments. She is suddenly startled by cries for help from the direction of the lavatory on this floor. They frighten her, and she crosses to the lavatory door.

GALINA: Tomas? I'm warning you [...] I'll report you to the police.

FEMALE VOICE *(Off)*: Help me, please! Please help me! Oh, God, h-e-e-lpp me!

GALINA: Oh, God. *(She tries the door, it is locked)* Oh, my God. You wait, please, wait.

She crosses the space to summon someone.

Khallo! Khelp [...] khelp, please. *(To herself)* My God, what am I going to do? *(More groaning)* Wait, please.

MARILYN MUNRO comes on. GALINA rushes to her.

GALINA: Oh, come, please. Come on.

MARYLYN: What is it? Where's the fire? *(Loses balance, momentarily)* Whoops. Guess you can tell where I've been. I'm not too bad, honest. Ooh, but I'm bursting for a wee.

GALINA: You come, please [...] *Toiletta.*

MARYLYN: That sums it up very nice, thanks. *(Pushing past her)* Excusez-nous. *(Tries the door)* Hey, it's locked! What'd you do with the key? The key...you know the key?

GALINA: Key, yes […] key.

MARYLYN: Well, I haven't got it. I asked you. Are you on your tod here? *(Louder)* Are you alone?

GALINA: You khelp, please.

MARYLYN: You help. S'pose you've no key to the cleaning cupboard either. Can't even provide you with a bucket. Oh, well […] s'pose you could say they brought it on themselves. *(Squats to urinate)*

GALINA: What are you doing, you idiot girl? *(Realizing)* N-o-o-o! Pig […] you […] get out.

MARYLYN: Who are you calling a pig? You probably bathe in the stuff. You think it matters a fuck to these people? Evelyn Parry, OBE […] soon to be Lady Parry. Mummy dearest. She keeps them this way! What'd you think gimme the idea? They'd just think it's one of the residents. And with no key to get at the nappies and the sluice buckets, they must want it this way, don't you think? I wouldn't worry about it, in any case. She's not paying you enough to bother. They keep em chained to the bed like howling inmates. *(On cue groaning)* You see? Might as well drop a biggie while I'm at it! *(Squats again)*

GALINA: You go now! *(Pushes her over)*

MARYLYN: You watch it […] or I'll shove your face through the door. Or I could bottle you to death for all the difference it'd make. You think anybody here cares a toss? And they couldn't where you come from…why else did you leave?

GALINA starts crying.

GALINA: Oh, Jesus. Forget about it, awright? I'll clean it up in the morning! *(Shouting)* When they let us have the fucking key! *(She leaves)*

GALINA gradually recovers herself […] crossing back to the toilet. She pounds several times on the door in frustration, then hears people approaching from another direction.

GALINA: He'll think it's me […] he'll say I did it […] he'll think it's me!

AMABEL: *(Approaching)* What's all this noise about, for God's sake? Everybody's asleep.

GALINA: *(Clinging to her)* It wasn't me, I swear to God […] this crazy girl came in and did it […] and somebody's in pain in the toilet […] I think she's dying.

AMABEL: *(Sees the mess)* What the bloody hell!

GALINA: *(Crying, on her knees)* I swear it wasn't me!

The Polish shop, that evening. A carnival atmosphere, corresponding to the opening scene, surrounds the occasion. More private party than off-licence opening, the occasion also resembles the impromptu factory lunch. ANIELA and STEFCIA are spreading a table. BEATA places sprigs of St John's Wart in their blouses. Ideally all three wear wreaths.

ANIELA: St John's Wart!

BEATA: Haven't you ever read Shakespeare? Evil spirits are more likely to be here than anywhere.

ANIELA: But where did you find it in England?

BEATA: My cousin in London.

ANIELA: Is he here? Is he coming tonight?

BEATA: They have their own celebrations. I don't really know who's coming.

STEFCIA: Anybody but the Russians.

ANIELA: That's a bit out of date, isn't it.

STEFCIA: Out of date? It was only last night.

BEATA: What's she talking about?

ANIELA: Her house guest.

STEFCIA: That's Russian, isn't it?

ANIELA: One Russian.

STEFCIA: How many do you know? And you've got to admit she was awful.

ANIELA: By your account, yes.

STEFCIA: And why should I lie? I wanted to like her. I was trying to get her to stay.

BEATA: Well, all right, what did she do?

STEFCIA: She stole from me, for a start.

ANIELA: Her husband.

BEATA: What!

STEFCIA: Not only that.

ANIELA: But mainly.

BEATA: Is he with her now?

STEFCIA: No!

BEATA: So she's meeting him later. They're running away together.

STEFCIA: Will you shut up.

ANIELA: She kicked her out.

BEATA: I don't want to carp, but that husband of yours is no saint.

STEFCIA: I didn't say he was.

ANIELA: You mean he approached you. Admit that he did, and Stef won't suspect you of anything.

STEFCIA: I know he did. That's all right.

BEATA: No, he didn't. That's not what I meant. But he asked if he could borrow some money, all right? I asked him what for, and he told me he needed to get back to Krakow for his mother's poor health.

ANIELA: What's wrong with that?

BEATA: *(To STEFCIA)* Was it true?

STEFCIA: No! His mother died years ago.

ANIELA: *(To BEATA)* How did you know?

BEATA: You don't ask a female friend of your wife for a loan. If you need to do that, then you're up to no good. And that's what I told him. *(To STEFCIA)* I hope you don't mind.

STEFCIA: Not at all. Now I know why he hates you.

ANIELA: So he won't be coming tonight.

STEFCIA: Up to his elbows in fish guts, who'd want him?

ANIELA: The Russian?

STEFCIA: *(To BEATA)* She stole my trust, to put it precisely. She asked for money and couldn't do the work. I always thought Russians were horses.

ANIELA: I know.

STEFCIA: Cheat you, all right, but at least they could work up a sweat. But this woman …

ANIELA: Lazy, eh?

STEFCIA: Comatose! Finally I put her to bed … and she snored the whole night! Gratitude, eh? I drove her to the town centre this morning, and she bit me goodbye.

ANIELA: What do you mean, bit?

STEFCIA: No, you're right. She gummed me goodbye […] toothless hag.

BEATA: Do you think that mayor and his aides will arrive? I baked apple duckling, just in case.

ANIELA: Why?

BEATA: What's the matter with you tonight? He's the mayor of a town, isn't he? Tonight is St John's Eve.

STEFCIA: She never heard of the Golden Duck.

ANIELA: Of course, I heard of it. Why make it for him, is all I meant.

STEFCIA: That's right. You think he cost us our jobs.

ANIELA: Nearly, he did.

BEATA: Well, I'm grateful. I hope he does come.

ANIELA: At least we're not likely to see her. She's married to English, so we're only scum.

BEATA: I met a lady policeman this morning. Walczewski, and she couldn't speak a word.

STEFCIA: That's not the mayor, is it?

She is referring to RADOST, coming into the light.

RADOST: I want to meet the woman who wounded my wife.

ANIELA: My God.

RADOST: You can understand me all right, can't you?

ANIELA: I can […] but it wasn't me.

BEATA: You're pathetic.

ANIELA: Well, why say it was?

BEATA: *(To RADOST)* It was none of us, all right? Leave us alone.

RADOST: Zubrowka!

BEATA: No, you've had enough.

RADOST: Isn't my accent clear?

ANIELA: You're the Russian!

RADOST: Lith-u-an-ian! I want to toast your day.

ANIELA: *(To STEFCIA)* You said the woman wasn't married!

BEATA: Idiot!

STEFCIA: I never said a thing!

RADOST: *(To STEFCIA)* Was it you? She says she slept in a cupboard!

STEFCIA: She snores!

RADOST: I know it! I sleep next door! *(Crooning)* Take care, pretty madam, be careful!

BEATA: *(To RADOST)* I told you, get out!

RADOST: *(Crooning)* You're spilling vodka all over my coat. *(Speech)* I can sing it to you just as well. *(Crooning)* I'll make you pay, oh, I'll never forgive you!

BEATA: *(Trying to shove him)* I'm serious […] you big oaf!

RADOST: *(Crooning)* Till I can kiss all your laughter away! *(Speech)* I'm not going to kiss any of you.

STEFCIA: Where's your wife now?

RADOST: Cleaning toilets. *(STEFCIA laughs)* What's wrong with that?

STEFCIA: That's just what she wouldn't do for me.

RADOST: Why should she?

STEFCIA: Why should she, that's right. I'm only a dirty Pole. I'm not English, after all, able to ask anything of dirty Russians.

RADOST: Lithuan—

STEFCIA: What do I care?

RADOST: What sort of business is it?

STEFCIA: Toilet business.

ANIELA: She tries to help people *(To STEFCIA)*, don't you.

STEFCIA: Somebody sent me your wife. She looked healthy. I thought she had her own teeth. I thought she could work as a dental assistant, like Aniela's hoping to be.

ANIELA: I haven't enough English.

STEFCIA: You ought to see his wife. The word for Exit is foreign to her.

RADOST: She made it to England alone.

STEFCIA: She couldn't work here and open her mouth.

RADOST: It's true. She's cleaning toilets.

BEATA: I don't want to rush you […]

RADOST: It's a party, no? D'you have any Golbaki? Pigeon pie?

BEATA: You're an unattached male.

RADOST: Baked duck?

BEATA: We're women alone in a strange country.

RADOST: But it's St John's Eve! Let's pretend I'm the unpaid cobbler, looking for the Golden Duck!

STEFCIA: I knew it. He's come to rob you.

BEATA: Police are watching us.

RADOST: You mistake me, I swear. I came here to wish you good luck.

BEATA: But this is a private party.

RADOST: *(Looking out)* So the people arriving right now, they're your guest?

BEATA: The shop's shut.

RADOST: No, it's not. *(Motioning to the audience)* What are they doing here?

BEATA: *(To ANIELA)* I told you to put the sign up – it says Closed. *(Looking out at the audience)* You no come. Home. You home.

She is addressing BRUNO BAGLIN and VICTORIA, who come on from the direction of the audience. BRUNO, like RADOST, shows signs of heavy drinking.

BRUNO: There's something I want you to do for me first. You owe it to me, in fact.

VICTORIA: They dunno what you're talking about.

BEATA: *(Showing sign)* Here […] here […] this!

BRUNO: I know that. I got a sign, too. *(Produces paper)* You see this? It's a notice I want you to put up.

VICTORIA: Let's get out of here, Bruno.

BRUNO: I want them to put this advert in their shop. Bruno Baglin, master builder. Any job you require. Any price you care to name. Do it.

BEATA: Only Polish here. You go.

BAGLIN: You go. Write it in Polish. Pretend I'm your brother-in-law. Like I'm desperate for work.

BEATA: *(Taking the card)* Now you go.

BRUNO: Now I watch you write it. I want to see it right there. *(Points in front of him)* Not on the top shelf […] And when your customers come in, I want you to point it out to them. Your friends will tell theirs […] and I'll never be hungry again.

RADOST steps forward.

RADOST: What are you telling to my wife?

Buzz of women reacting to this.

BRUNO: That's all right, mate. Curse me a blue streak. Are you a builder? Any hopes of being a builder?

RADOST: If you threaten her, I'll call the police. You go now. Outside.

BEATA: This has nothing to do with you.

BRUNO: If I saw you being a builder, I'd slit your fucking throat. *(Produces knife)* With this.

The women gasp.

BEATA: Now see what you did? You got him angry.

RADOST: Don't worry, I'd take it off him no worries.

BEATA: No! *(Stepping between them)* You're not going to do a thing to him. You want to get us deported?

RADOST: But he threatened you.

BEATA: Like I've never been threatened before? Our bandits carried bayonets in their teeth.

VICTORIA: Bruno, will you come on. It's late, and the pubs will be spewing up, and I ent looking to get squashed between the tossers and the bleeding fuzz. And put that damn thing away. *(To the group)* He's not going to hurt anybody.

ANIELA: *(Crossing to her)* You come over here, dear […] away from that maniac.

VICTORIA: No, I'm all right, thanks.

BRUNO: Don't you touch her.

VICTORIA: Bruno, will you shut up?

BRUNO: Yeah, all right. Everything's cool, see? I put it away.

ANIELA: Have some food, please. Polish duck. *(Motioning her)* Have […]have.

VICTORIA: *(To BRUNO)* I don't want to offend them.

ANIELA: In Poland there is the famous legend about the Golden Duck.

STEFCIA: Will you shut up about that duck?

ANIELA: You said I didn't know about it.

BEATA: She can't understand anyway.

ANIELA: *(As she serves VICTORIA a portion of duck)* It is story about foreign army in palace […] and duck […] magic duck save people. Our country final save.

BRUNO: Yeah, the duck that laid the golden egg […] job lot of tickets to England. *(Grabbing Victoria)* Come on out of it.

RADOST: *(Stepping in)* You let her finish the story!

STEFCIA: Oh, God, now look. He'll pull the knife again.

BEATA: Well, get it away from him.

RADOST: *(Rushing in)* Bastaaard!

RADOST gets BRUNO'S head in an arm lock and drags him out to the street. VICTORIA and the other women follow, and there's a piercing scream, which seems to unleash a frenzied commotion in the street in a grotesque parody of the opening scene.

Characters do a reprise almost as in a musical finale.

VICTORIA: *(Off)* I want you to leave us alone, get it?

Bottle breaking.

PCSO: Did anybody actually see what happened? I understand a serious fight broke out in the Polish shop. *(Spotting BEATA)* You. I warned you about trouble this morning.

BEATA: Trouble? No trouble.

STEFCIA: Tell her the shop was shut.

GALINA, EVELYN and AMABEL approach.

ANIELA: You have to tell her about the crippled girl […] I'm sure she's been hurt.

BEATA: How exactly do I do that?

GALINA: *(Overlapping, at STEFCIA)* You did something bad to my husband.

AMABEL: I'm sorry, Mrs P. I didn't know who else to ring. She was going ballistic at the Centre, like I was blaming her.

EVELYN: It's all right. I'm glad to help. Only what's she doing here?

ANIELA: *(To BEATA)* Tell her!

BEATA: All right! *(To PCS0)* Girl […] bad leg […] bad things happen.

PCSO: What's she talking about? What girl?

KIERA and JEN approach.

KIERA: I seen what happened […] I seen it all.

PSCO: So *you're* the girl?

JEN: She's just creating, officer. She ent seen a blessed thing.

PSCO   *(To JEN)* Just a minute, love. *(Taking hold of KIERA)* Is this the girl you mean?

KIERA: It isn't me!

JEN: I tell you she's having a wind-up.

PAULINE: *(Approaching)* Someone told me my tenants have been in a fight.

AMABEL: What are *you* doing here, love?

PCSO: *(Grabbing PAULINE)* Is this the one?

EVELYN: Excuse me, she seems to think her husband's been hurt.

PCSO: *(On the verge of losing it)* I'm trying to conduct an inquiring! *(Recognizing her)* You again […] with her! Don't you ever go home?

Now LAUREN approaches.

LAUREN: Somebody said there's been a murder? BBC here. Has somebody done something violent? I've a right to know.

Everyone speaks. In the general mayhem VICTORIA and RADOST pass unnoticed some distance away.

EVELYN: No, wait. You're not going to broadcast this, are you […] with her standing there?

They disappear momentarily as the WACLAV party approach the cemetery. When RADOST and VICTORIA reappear, they are counters from an earlier era.

WACLAV: This […] this is the place. I know it. This is where we were camped.

STELLA: What's he so excited about?

CAROLE: He said this is the place. *(To WACLAV)* Are you sure? This is the local cemetery.

STELLA: God, no. My husband will think I'm seeing someone.

WACLAV: Sure, yes. This where they die.

STELLA: Dunno what I'm doing at a midnight vigil. We don't believe in that sort of thing.

CAROLE: At least he's not being belligerent.

WACLAV: Shh. We pray, eh? We pray.

There is a sudden hush as they watch the final exchange. RADOST is featured as a post-war labourer; VICTORIA as a wartime resident.

VICTORIA: We was known evermore as the Alphabet Brigade [...] the GI Brides and the POW scrubbers, and most never knew which was which. We all said we was headed for Get-Rich-Quick, Arizona, and nobody never checked on the truth. We all hoped we'd never return anyway. That's why we did it. *(To RADOST)* You worked here a long time, have you[...]long time?

RADOST: Oh, yes, a very long time.

VICTORIA: My God. You speak English. I was just larking about.

RADOST: You wish me to leave you?

VICTORIA: Oh, no! I'm glad we can talk [...] I was thinking we wouldn't be able. No, this is smashing. Look, my names Victoria Sponge [...] that's a cream cake in England, but it also happens to be my name. And yours is [...]?

RADOST: Radost Waclav.

VICTORIA: I'll have to practise that one. D'you get enough to eat? I mean I know none of us do nowadays. That's part of what they call the victory. But at least they don't starve you nor nothing [...] beat you.

RADOST: I am all right.

VICTORIA: Do you mind if I ast you something? *(He nods)* What do you know about a Golden Duck?

RADOST: Who told you about that?

VICTORIA: It was just something I heard about the other day. Is it some kind of secret or something?

RADOST: That's right. A legend everyone knows but never repeats.

VICTORIA: On pain of death? Don't repeat it to me then [...] if it's cursed.

RADOST: After centuries of foreign invasion of Poland, the Royal Palace was said to hold a huge fortune in the cellar, guarded by a Golden Duck. Some claimed it was an evil spirit, the devil in benign form. Others said it had magical powers and would bestow good fortune on anyone who caught a glimpse. But no one was ever quite sure. And no one ever wanted to find out, in case it really was the devil and cast a spell that would linger for centuries more. Sooner or later, someone was bound to find out. And he happened to be a poor cobbler, fired from his job and wandering the streets for days. He entered the palace alone, stayed there overnight. It was St John's Eve!

VICTORIA: I'm beginning to get this!

RADOST: Next morning, with everyone watching, the cobbler emerged, thunderstruck. Some thought him bewitched, assuming the duck was the devil, that town, as a result, was doomed. But then he spoke, of a wondrous transformation – the duck was a beautiful maiden, whose gift was a limitless fortune, on condition the town remained pure [...] free of foreign invasion. No one could marry a foreigner. They were even discouraged from entering the town.

VICTORIA: So who am I, the foreign invader?

RADOST: We've invaded you.

VICTORIA: If that's what beaten and starved means.

RADOST: No, this is where the new town will be located. They'll build the future here. Did you sustain injury?

VICTORIA: Did I what? No, no, I always had this [...] since a child anyway.

RADOST: Poor child.

VICTORIA: Yeah, they don't think so. They think because it isn't a war wound it doesn't exist [...] or I don't deserve no more consideration. I think I deserve it same as before [...] it didn't go away, did it? I'm no better off. *(A beat)* I wish I could get you something to eat [...] some Victoria Sponge. Ha-ha. I wouldn't ask you to marry a foreigner. But we could visit here now and again. Just the two of us, in private.

RADOST: Of course.

VICTORIA: Yeah, long as nobody knows [...] Our secret, eh?

Final fade.

Brides, Bombs and Boardrooms

Performed by second-year Drama students of Exeter University under the direction of Martin Harvey on 19 May 2009.

MINNY PLAYFAIR	Rachel Gregory
PRUNELLA	Hanna Gregson
LOVEDAY OGDEN	Rebecca Benzie
WALTER	Ewan Goddard, Thomas Angell
LISA	Rosanna Elliott, Amy Kinsella
STEWART OGDEN	Andy Vyse
AUNT HENNY	Hannah Mawditt
JANIS UPSHAW	Laura Hollis
STEPHANIE NOUN	Katie Webber
GINA	Phillipa Cole
JAMEELA	Katherine Brooks
YELENA	Annie Wessman
TAMARA	Camilla Jones
HAMID	Jack Truss
FARIDA	Maria Lancaster
BUBENOV	Matt Weigold
VORONIN	Scott Crampes
BETTY THOMAS	Jessica Wood

Middle England

Katherine Brooks, Ewan Goddard and Rosanna Elliott in hospital scene from *Brides, Bombs and Boardrooms*.

Amy Kinsella and Annie Wessman consider mother–daughter fate in *Brides, Bombs and Boardrooms*.

Thomas Angell delivers final curse in *Brides, Bombs and Boardrooms*.

MINNY PLAYFAIR, compèring the action, addresses the audience:

MINNY: Erm, thank you. Good evening. I'd like to welcome you all to a different kind of event. This isn't reality television. It isn't the *Strictly Come Dancing* final or *Celebrity* what-have-you. There aren't any prizes on offer if you ring a certain telephone number with the correct answer. But I think I can promise you more than you bargained for, which is some claim to make considering all that we're not going to give you. You're going to take part in a public inquiry into an event that concerns us all – and no, this isn't a party political broadcast about the next general election. I'm not sure, in fact, how it's going to end. But if you'll bear with me just a bit, I think you'll begin to catch on. We begin here, I suppose, in this shamelessly middle-class household. But, if you look closely, you'll see something I genuinely don't think you expected, whatever you might of […] I was about to say people like that. But that's the point. Have you ever met anybody like them?

Unit set in which the various scenes take place with minimal, rapid changes. This opening features WALTER, LOVEDAY, PRUNELLA and, momentarily, the offstage sound of someone retching. WALTER is somewhat disabled. It is a family home somewhere in Greater London.

PRUNELLA: Better by far if you'd said you were queer […] then we'd know what we're up against.

LOVEDAY: They call it gay now, Mater.

PRUNELLA: I call it a clear case of don't-ask-me-what […] wilful deception?

WALTER: We're legally married.

PRUNELLA: That's just what I mean. Did we know […] did you bother to tell anyone?

LOVEDAY: This was more than a first date.

PRUNELLA: No, unfortunately, I don't think it was. He met the girl, told her about us, offered us to her, and then […] *she* told *him*. *(To WALTER)* Did she even bother to call you good looking?

LOVEDAY: He'll say she's too honest for that.

PRUNELLA: Naturally. 'I couldn't possibly want you for anything else. Please open accounts in my name'.

WALTER: There's no point in talking with either of you.

LOVEDAY: What did you want us to say – She's adorable […] we hope you'll be happy together? Not a chance, mate.

PRUNELLA: I haven't quite finished what I have to say. *(To WALTER)* Did you really expect us to let you spit on your sister like that?

WALTER: This has nothing to do with—

PRUNELLA: Yes, unfortunately, it has […] if you continue to work at the family job. And don't bother to say you haven't told her about us.

LOVEDAY: Didn't need to – she looked us up.

WALTER: She'll be an asset.

LOVEDAY: You see there? He gave her a job.

WALTER: Piss off.

PRUNELLA: That'll do now, both of you. *(Beat)* I want you to listen to Loveday, Walter, she may speak from more than mere spite.

LOVEDAY: What the mater is saying is simply this: you didn't consult us on anything, did you? You've secretly married a Russian. Why secret? You know she must want something.

PRUNELLA: Grandfather Cotter was prey to one swindling attempt after another. Markby and Unwin constantly took up the cudgels on our behalf.

LOVEDAY: And your bride comes from Thieves' Paradise. You didn't court, you know nothing about her.

WALTER: She's been very poor all her life.

LOVEDAY: And had dreams of becoming very rich. We know.

PRUNELLA: It's a classic scenario – don't think she's the first.

WALTER: I don't, but just look at her. She's a featherweight. She's in there chucking up!

LOVEDAY: You don't suppose she caught a form of swine 'flu, do you?

WALTER: In that case, she'll die […] you'll be through with her within the week.

PRUNELLA: What Loveday is saying, darling, is […]

WALTER: […] exactly what she said. Do you think she could be any more explicit?

PRUNELLA: Possibly not, but you could be misinterpreting her, is that possible?

LOVEDAY: At least concede that you're vulnerable.

WALTER: How anti-this marriage are you? Just tell me that.

LOVEDAY: How much can you bear?

PRUNELLA: If you'd come to *announce your intention […]*

WALTER: You'd have shot it down. That's exactly why we did it this way.

LOVEDAY: Well, then don't come to us for a handout. Business and sentiment don't often mix, dear. You proved that for us when you lost all that money the first time. Now you want to prove it again with this stranger? The least you could have had was tact […] told us she already had a job.

WALTER: You'd have seen through that as well.

LOVEDAY: Mater, you talk to him. I'll only get angrier.

PRUNELLA: Perhaps if you'd told us one at a time […]

WALTER: *(To LOVEDAY)* You can marry Stewart, and you can get him a job with the firm, of course.

LOVEDAY: Of course. He's the reason we're sitting so pretty […] you in particular.

WALTER: I don't need to hear how that bastard is my life support.

LOVEDAY: *He's* the reason you still have a job. *(Stops him)* All right, I wasn't going to rub it in. But – damn-it-all – you provoke it from me, as though you *wanted* it.

PRUNELLA: Nobody likes belittling you, darling. You begin to resemble Tiny Tim. But you don't have the history that inspires confidence.

LOVEDAY: How much did you lose on the futures market?

WALTER: All right, kick me out of the business.

PRUNELLA: We can't do that. You're my son, we're a reputable family, and your condition is potentially scandalous. We'd never hear the end of it.

Sound of toilet flushing.

PRUNELLA: Sounds like she's coming up for air.

WALTER: Well, look, neither of you say anything, please […] at least till she's been here awhile. She's tongue-tied.

PRUNELLA: Perhaps she knows a word or two of French.

WALTER: She speaks English – that's not the point.

LISA appears, bird-like, embarrassed.

WALTER: Mother […] Loveday? This is Lisa.

LISA: I […] very sorry.

PRUNELLA: Yes, you must feel positively wretched.

LISA: Little better […] thank you.

PRUNELLA: If I was sick in front of absolute strangers, I know I'd want to perish. You couldn't dig me a hole deep enough.

LOVEDAY: Something you ate on the plane, was it? Or something you caught earlier.

LISA: I don't know. I ate very little.

WALTER: And we arrived here directly from France.

PRUNELLA: Good Lord, a French registry office.

LOVEDAY: Too right you caught a disease.

WALTER: It wasn't the French form of Avian 'flu, for God's sake. We were up at 4.30. Poor girl's bushwacked.

LOVEDAY: All right, but it's got to be something.

PRUNELLA: And you shouldn't put more on your stomach, my dear.

WALTER: Are you saying you're not going to feed us?

LOVEDAY: She couldn't keep it down.

LISA: She's right, I don't want anything.

PRUNELLA: Perhaps yogurt's the best thing.

WALTER: Lisa's your daughter-in-law, for God's sake. You can run to more than a yogurt pot for her.

LOVEDAY: We know who she is, thank you.

PRUNELLA: And that's not all she's ever going to eat. Good Lord, did you think she was going to be chained in the cellar or something? How Dickensian. *(To LISA)* Charles Dickens, my dear. Your husband thinks we're putting you into the workhouse, on bread and gruel.

LISA: I told you I don't want nothing.

WALTER: Would you like to lie down?

LOVEDAY: You're both going to live in your old room, is that the plan?

WALTER: We're looking at a flat near the marina.

LOVEDAY: On your meagre crust? Has she got a private income? *(To LISA)* You better know it now, love. We keep Walter here on a very short rein […] for the best of all reasons. You see he cost the family millions one time, through sheer carelessness.

WALTER: She doesn't need any of this.

LOVEDAY: I'd want to know […] if I was starting out. I'd almost call it his job to tell me, his calling.

LISA: You're going too fast for me, both of you.

PRUNELLA: Indeed, yes, you both need to unwind. Spend time together. When exactly did it happen?

LISA: Five days ago […] in Paris.

LOVEDAY: So you live in France.

LISA: I came there from Russia, one month ago. The place where I was she was […] *(To Walter) ouzhazna.*

WALTER: Horrible. We met over the Internet, all right? I'm not a paedophile […] she's over 21.

PRUNELLA: And perfectly charming, I know, we can see. What Loveday is saying, I'm sure, has to do with your circumstance.

LOVEDAY: Are you able to work? If you lived in France, it's no problem.

LISA: Why?

WALTER: *(Overlapping)* Her visa is tourist, all right? For six months.

PRUNELLA: It's all right for us, dear. But what about you … if you're separated?

LOVEDAY: […] your particular skills. If you were living in France, there'd be no problem. You'd stay here as part of the EU.

LISA: The what?

WALTER: She has a degree in accounting, advanced business.

A beat.

LOVEDAY: She's looking to us to support her. That's it. She wants a job. She knows she can't get it through channels.

WALTER: Back off.

LOVEDAY: Look at Mum and say that's not what she wants. Deny it to your mother.

STEWART OGDEN appears.

STEWART: You're all here – great. Walter, this concerns you, too. Pay attention. *(Looks at LISA but does not really acknowledge her)* There's been a serious hostile bid.

PRUNELLA: What did I tell you? *(To STEWART)* Get onto Joshua Markby. He'll know exactly what needs to be done.

LOVEDAY: Stewart's in charge now, Mater. You say serious – how so?

STEWART: Well, they got hold of the quarterly trade figures, saw our shares plummet, purchased a huge volume of bonds from the bank […] we had to expect it, really.

PRUNELLA: Who is it, British company?

LOVEDAY: Oh, it wouldn't matter if they were, ultimately, Japanese. *(To STEWART)* Who do you have in mind for the rival bid?

STEWART: No one. You don't want control out of the family, do you. We're going to issue a load of dual-credit stock […] *(To PRUNELLA)* Shares that are worth less than yours so they can't get a seat on the board. Even with only 4 percent stock, you'd still own 52 percent of the company. We need, though, to buy Walter out.

PRUNELLA: I don't understand. We own much more than four percent, Stewart. What are you talking about?

STEWART: Oh, God, yes. I'm saying if. Hypothetically, on paper. If your stock options amounted to only a total of four percent, you'd still have control, because they're worth more than everyone else's.

WALTER: More than mine, for example.

STEWART: Technically, yes, but at our price, you can afford to retire.

PRUNELLA: What if we were to give Lisa the money? *(To LISA)* You'd accept that, wouldn't you, dear.

WALTER: You mean you're giving it to us as a wedding present?

PRUNELLA: I mean we're giving it to her.

STEWART: I don't get this. What's going on? Walter's gone and got himself married?

LOVEDAY: To a Russian, no less.

PRUNELLA: Do you think she could be behind the takeover bid?

WALTER: She has no money! And why are you talking in front of her?

STEWART: You didn't go and give them a wedding present, did you?

LOVEDAY: We don't exactly approve of the match.

PRUNELLA: We didn't exactly know about it. That's the point. Walter disappears on a holiday weekend. When he comes back, I have a daughter-in-law! Wouldn't you expect me to be a little irate? *(To LISA)* No matter who it was?

STEWART: I'm afraid you're going to be a bit more than that. But I don't exactly know how to broach this. I mean it explains the thing perfectly. Walt gets married, he wants to set himself and his bride in a new house [...] Only if you didn't authorize anything ...

LOVEDAY: We didn't know about it!

PRUNELLA: Just what are you getting at now, Stewart?

STEWART: Well, it isn't only the takeover. I had a call from Ewald and Renfrew Estate Agents about an offer on a property of theirs. Apparently someone had offered them shares of our stock against the cost of the house.

LOVEDAY: *(To WALTER)* You lunatic!

STEWART: Naturally I denied the claim. Apart from anything else, it's absolutely against stock market procedure to sell stock in this way without the approval of shareholders. Walt would have been criminally liable.

LOVEDAY: You perfect bastard. *You're* responsible for our shares going down [...] again!

STEWART: I don't think so, at least directly. But I honestly think it's time Walt stepped down as a company director.

LOVEDAY: Oh, don't worry, we'll make him.

STEWART: If this got out, of course, he'd *have* to resign.

LOVEDAY: Oh, lock him up [...] I mean in an institution!

WALTER: You can't do that – I'm not criminal or crazy.

STEWART: But you did try to sell the shares.

WALTER: Nothing's signed one way or another. I'll give you my signature now, though, triumphantly. You think I ever wanted to be part of this three-ring fire sale?

PRUNELLA: Now you're just being an infant.

LOVEDAY: Stewart's right though, Mater.

PRUNELLA: I told you – you can't walk out of this family. Now we'll make this young woman a generous offer [...] see she's safely on her way home [...]

WALTER: And you'll see us next when you can find us. *(To LISA)* Let's go.

AUNT HENNY comes on.

AUNT HENNY: Hallo, Walter! I came here hoping you'd be back. How was it […] whatever it was?

WALTER: Go piss up a rope.

MINNY: This is Walter's aunt Henny, supposedly his family favourite.

AUNT HENNY: I thought perhaps I'd treat us all to a pub lunch somewhere like Henley, but I see now we're more than a carload. How many of us have cars? *(No answer)* This really is the ideal day for it. We might even have a punt, those of us feeling inclined. I've been so remiss about seeing you all. I don't even remember birthdays anymore. And of course, I wouldn't blame you if you didn't even ask me to sit down. But I wanted to show you my heart's in the proper aorta. Prunnie, please tell me, what's going on? Why's my nephew got something like spite on his face? Have you been martyring him again?

MINNY introduces the next scene.

MINNY: Be honest now. Was that what you expected, even if you didn't really relate to the situation? The family are rich, after all. What claim have they got on anyone's sympathy? You can answer that for yourselves after watching this next scene. Walter and Lisa have gone decidedly down-market, to a two-star B and B. They've thrown themselves, as it were, on the council.

Room in a bed and breakfast. WALTER and LISA are being interviewed by JANIS UPSHAW and STEPHANIE NOUN independently, though their conversations will overlap. They arrive together.

JANIS: Good God, you're not from Weatherborough Council, are you?

STEPHIE: Stone and Pettigrew […] solicitors. My name is—

JANIS: Thank God. This is almost my first day. I thought perhaps they were checking up on me. I'm here to help a disabled man find permanent accommodation.

STEPHIE: Immigration case, mine. Russian woman.

JANIS: It's not likely they're related then, are they.

STEPHIE: I shouldn't think so.

JANIS: Four. Who are you?

STEPHIE: Four.

JANIS: Curiouser and curiouser.

STEPHIE: Mrs Lisa Regis […] married to Walter Regis?

JANIS: Walter Regis is the one I want. Well, then they are related.

WALTER: And we're both here, don't worry. Come in, both of you.

STEPHIE: I don't see how this is going to work. Perhaps if you'd ring my assistant for another appointment. I was making this house call specially.

WALTER: What's your name? I just rang Stone and […]

STEPHIE: *(Handing him card)* Oh, yes. It's a funny one – Stephanie Noun. Everyone calls me Stephie as well, like the tennis star. You just ring Mandy for some day next week.

LISA: But we cannot. *Ne vos mazhna.* I have was kick out now!

JANIS: *(To WALTER)* And you'll have to go down to council HQ. We're not your convenience, you know. You told us severely disabled.

WALTER: I'm disabled. Look. *(He demonstrates)*

JANIS: That's genuine, is it? We're on the lookout for benefit cheats.

WALTER: I've nothing to hide. I've nothing, full stop. Ask my missus.

JANIS: […] who just happens to be an illegal alien.

LISA: I am not illegal.

STEPHIE: But you say you've exceeded your visitor's visa. *(Interrupts her protest)* There's no desperate rush. They're not going to escort you out in the morning. The worst they could do is place you in a detention centre, but you're a lone woman, so it's not likely.

LISA: Ah-ha. Like a prison, you mean.

WALTER: And we're married [...] I'm British.

STEPHIE: But you're also applying for free legal aid. That could pose a problem.

WALTER: It's like I was going to say to this lady [...]

JANIS: Janis Upshaw.

WALTER: [...] my bank account's been frozen, all my assets seized.

STEPHIE: And they're going to want to know why.

WALTER: Do you offer legal aid or not? That's all we need to know.

STEPHIE: Oh, we'll plead your case, don't worry. That's what I do [...] at least my associates will if it gets before a judge. I don't want to leave you with any false hopes, that's all. You appear to be bankrupt [...]

WALTER: [...]I'm not.

STEPHIE: [...] and your wife's non-EU. She's supposed to have a skill.

WALTER: You've heard her English.

STEPHIE: But can she speak Scouse, for example? *(To LISA)* [...] or know where a Geordie comes from? Believe it or not, those are actually on the new citizenship test.

WALTER: She doesn't want a passport.

STEPHIE: What I'm saying is, she wants a job. The citizen test may be barmy, but it's English as is spoke [...] in the street, in the workplace, where she wants to be. *(To LISA)* Is that right?

JANIS: If she's working, I'm not sure you qualify for housing.

WALTER: She's not working.

LISA: They kick me out!!

STEPHIE: You've a right of appeal first. Let's start with that. *(Gets out his notebook)* You married when?

JANIS: Think we might be after the same information. *(Gets out her housing form)* Is it all right if I ask a question or two?

STEPHIE: What, exactly?

JANIS: Oh, only if something comes up. You carry on. I'll let you know.

STEPHIE: Well, all right, when were you married?

LISA: In Paris.

WALTER: Two months ago.

STEPHIE: That doesn't sound quite right. A visitor's visa is usually for six. Are you sure they asked you to leave?

WALTER: They'll cart her off sooner or later. Can you stop them?

STEPHIE: Yes, I tell you I will try. But this is a two-star B and B […] and you're applying for benefit […] those aren't the highest assets.

WALTER: Can't you say I'm a company director? I've got proof.

JANIS: *(Beginning to close the forms)* If you are, I dunno what I'm doing here.

WALTER: I was voted off. It's not a scam. All my assets were frozen. Took the flat back.

JANIS: Why? Are you a white collar criminal? They discovered you cooking the books?

LISA: Who is criminal, Walter? His own mother kick him out!

JANIS: I don't understand – it's a family firm? You've been a naughty boy?

LISA: Naughty, yes. He marry with me. Dirty Russian.

JANIS: You're not serious.

WALTER: My family believe in fortress Britain, you see, and a lady from the Evil Empire, well, she's worse than Scheherazade.

JANIS: But they ought to be grateful. I mean in your condition [...] well, it's not to everyone's taste, if you'll pardon my bluntness.

WALTER: Not at all. They felt exactly the same.

JANIS: Well, there you are! What went wrong?

WALTER: No woman could possibly want me without money [...] so they took it away from me.

JANIS: Oh, I see. Oh, you poor man.

STEPHIE begins with LISA.

STEPHIE: They operate on a point system now. So many points gains admission. Fifty points for a Ph.D. [...] skills the qualified national lacks. *(Beat)* You're not getting this, are you. If you had a job in a bank, say, with connections to the new Russia [...]

LISA: I hate the new Russia. *(Fakes spitting)* Phoo, *blin*. I want away.

STEPHIE: I was afraid of that. You're not French, are you, coming from Paris? If you lived there, maybe you're part of the Union.

LISA: I never want to hear part-of-union again. I married to British.

STEPHIE: That no longer counts, with all the new immigrants from the Union [...]

LISA: Ahh!

STEPHIE: All right! *(To WALTER)* Explain to her this is for nothing. She ought at least to be polite.

LISA: You give us nothing. *(Holds up letter)* Here. Home Office give us this.

STEPHIE: I'll take care of that.

LISA: What in hell you doing? I don't trust nobody.

STEPHIE: I'm going to write to them, for God's sake.

LISA: God's sakes you'll send me to jail. I don't trust nobody […] nowhere. *(Starts to weep)*

JANIS: *(Noticing)* Oh, blisters! What is it, female trouble?

LISA: *(Through tears in Russian)* My father just died of stomach cancer […] my mother's diabetic. Hospital sent her home without treatment […] and my brother steals!

STEPHIE: We can't manipulate the law, even when it's patently unfair.

JANIS: *(Arm round LISA)* Let's just get you a tissue. *(To STEPHIE)* Yours is a brutal profession.

STEPHIE: That's why they employ me. Don't think I don't care. One girl I'm trying to help is virtually living off me. From Mogadishu. Whole family except for an aunt was wiped out by Al Qaeda troops […] and they'd have killed her if she hadn't escaped. And what's the reason she can't gain asylum to live with the aunt? She's suspected of being Al Qaeda. I've even got someone in Cherie Blair's office to plead her case.

JANIS: And my parents hated my brother-in-law. My father swore he was part of the real IRA … refused to toast the ceremony even.

STEPHIE: What are you talking about? What's that to do with anything?

JANIS: Nothing at all, I suppose. I'm trying to […] just say how I understand what this poor boy is going through with his family.

STEPHIE: Well, don't split your […] infinitives over it.

JANIS: I'm going to try to help him […]

STEPHIE: […] and I tell you I'm trying to help her, somehow. When you're finished with him […]

JANIS: Oh, the whole form is 30-odd pages. We'll be here for ages yet, especially if I need to ask her anything.

STEPHIE: I only ask because […]

JANIS: […] you're as anxious to help them as I am. I can see it in your face.

STEPHIE: Force of habit, I'm afraid. We need to disguise our emotions.

JANIS: You do that brilliantly.

STEPHIE: Do you mind please? My time's short, and I need to ask him some questions.

JANIS: This is hardly going to take all day.

STEPHIE: I haven't got more than an hour!

JANIS: All right. I'll be as quick as I can. Only this is almost my first day at work […]

STEPHIE: You already told me that.

JANIS: You wouldn't want *your* staff to do things in half measures, would you? I can see in your […] determined eye.

STEPHIE: I'll come back after lunch.

WALTER: Having reduced my wife to tears?

STEPHIE: Make her understand, will you, and you, please, understand. There's only so much you can do, in a case like this.

WALTER: You can or I can […] which is it?

STEPHIE: Anybody. I've cited you the best case I know for asylum, and that's due to go down the Sewanee, and yours is several degrees worse. Between hopeful and no hope, you're hovering somewhere round beside-the-point. And don't even contemplate slipping in between the cracks. *I* couldn't be party to that, but you'd never get away with it, as others have found to their cost.

WALTER: I haven't asked for that, have I?

STEPHIE: Like saying she has an executive job when she hasn't. They'll want affidavits[…] testimonials from her employers. You say you don't work?

WALTER: My family made that impossible […] because of Lisa.

STEPHIE: *(After a beat)* We'll draft a letter to say you're an […] invalid. Your GP will write in support. You need your wife here to look after you, how's that?

JANIS: And I'm sure she could claim care allowance.

STEPHIE: Good God, don't do that […] at least until we've submitted something.

JANIS: Well, they don't have to own up to everything, do they? I'm for everyone claiming as much as they can, to be frank with you. I took this when my Morris was injured himself in a road accident […] and you'd think we're entitled to everything going. The rival insurers with their no-claims crooks (excuse me) ended up proving it was our fault. Morris was driving without due care and attention. And now he can barely walk. He has whatever they'll give him, and no, he's not playing golf or making charity walks on the side. I wanted children, and now I've got him. *(To LISA)* You claim what you can, love, with our blessing. I'm here to help anyone who's entitled.

STEPHIE: I don't think there's much more to be done for the moment.

JANIS: I shouldn't be very much longer, myself […] It too is on a point system, but I'll give this the highest recommendation, call it urgent, well, yes, it's a B and B.

STEPHIE: I've got to be going, in any case. *(Opens door, finding GINA CORDOVAN outside)* Pardon me.

GINA: Did you just say you're from Immigration?

STEPHIE: No, I didn't.

GINA: But you said […]

STEPHIE: Are you spying on these people? I'm an Immigration solicitor, but that's quite different […]

GINA: Doesn't matter.

STEPHIE: And my caseload is full at the moment, sorry.

GINA: They've still got to leave.

STEPHIE: What? Now wait a minute. They're not illegal. Mrs Regis has a perfectly valid visa […]

GINA: I don't care. I don't care what you're telling me. They've got to get out of here.

WALTER: But we paid to the end of the month.

GINA: Don't worry, I'll give it you back. Give it all back. You can call it my newlywed gift. Happy landings and all that.

STEPHIE: What's going on here?

GINA: He never said they weren't English.

STEPHIE: […] Oh, for God's sake.

JANIS: *(Overlapping)* But that's monstrous.

WALTER: […] I am English.

GINA: I told you. He said they're on the honeymoon, and I said all right. I never knew the police would be after you.

STEPHIE: I'd better warn you – they'll be after you. Kick them out, go ahead. It'll only end in your closing down. Racial discrimination.

JANIS: Especially when I add my report about sub-standard conditions.

GINA: Don't you get it? I'm frightened to death.

WALTER: I'm disabled.

STEPHIE: They're both harmless.

GINA: No, you don't understand. The Mabutu family came here three months ago. If you were here, you probably heard about it. It spread like an oil slick over the local news.

STEPHIE: I remember. They lost their appeal in the end.

GINA: That's right. And the next morning four beer-barrelled constables dragged papa and mama and three screaming kids off in a curtained maria somewhere […] never to be seen again.

STEPHIE: I happen to know. That's not at all how it works.

GINA: How do you know? You weren't here.

STEPHIE: But as you say, it was on the television. They were taken to Heathrow discreetly […] filmed at the airport, boarding the plane.

GINA: Yeah, and murdered the next day in their beds.

JANIS: How appalling!

STEPHIE: Never happened.

GINA: I don't care. Other residents began blaming me. Said I'd informed on them […] placed a curse. And that's plainly not true.

STEPHIE: Of course not, but […]

GINA: I wasn't the one with the powers, but someone is, someone did it to them. I accept they didn't voodoo themselves.

STEPHIE: Are you serious?

JANIS: I don't understand.

GINA: More fool you if you think I'm not.

STEPHIE: They asked for asylum and failed […]

GINA: […] yeah, and paid the ultimate price. That's exactly why they failed. They were cursed. Nobody believed them, of course. And now the curse moves on […]

to anybody that was ever friendly to them. My old mum caved in a month after they left. Then my husband went totally blind. They're sparing me just to make me suffer more. But soon someone's going to fall and break their neck.

STEPHIE: The timbers are rotten.

GINA: My twin sister's developed ovarian cancer. That shows how I'm marked. *(To WALTER, perhaps pointing)* You can't walk as well as you did. *(To the others)* As late as last Thursday he was bounding up and down the stairs with trays of food for his beloved. Soon she'll have to spoon-feed him!

WALTER: She's confusing me with another person.

GINA: That's right, the person you were. You can't even remember yourself. *(Crossing to LISA)* I'm not being ghoulish and spiteful, my dear. It's for your own […] survival. I'm attempting to save your life.

LISA: I don't understand you are saying.

JANIS: This has all turned a shade hysterical suddenly. I think we should all […] *(Takes a deep breath)*

STEPHIE: You talk as though some horrible murder had been committed here […] that they're somehow under its spell.

GINA: Exactly. They'll soon have to carry him out, and I'm not going to be held responsible. The voodoo priests have tormented me enough.

JANIS: Well, now look. I'm not what you'd call a reactive person. But even if we act expeditiously here, the soonest I can move on this is two to three weeks. *(To GINA)* We're talking the rest of their lives.

GINA: The priests also move expeditiously […] in a matter of hours. They're also talking the rest of their lives.

STEPHIE: All right, hang on here. The answer's simple, you know? There's your rebate – you just shift hotels. *(To GINA)* Would that be enough to placate the gods, do you think?

GINA: […] priests.

STEPHIE: Oh, shit, I've offended them now.

JANIS'S mobile phone rings.

JANIS: No doubt that's my office. I'll set the wheels in motion. *(Responding)* Janis Stephie. Oh, shit, I mean Upshaw. O-h-h. This is me, yes. Go ahead. Yes, I'm with them both right now. They're newly married. And there seems to be some urgency, but don't ask me to explain right now. It's too complicated. No, no children, but [...]That's right, Walter Regis and his bride. He's disabled, severely. Maximum points, I should think. I'd like to be able to help them as soon as [...] Yes, Regis, Walter Regis [...] What's that? I promise you he's disabled. Cannot walk unassisted [...] Oh, but surely that can't mean [...] That's ridic [...] that's utterly [...] I'm, well, I'm dumbfounded [...] Yes, I'll tell them. Then I'll come straight [...] *(Stops short, waiting seconds before speaking again)*

STEPHIE: That was your office, was it?

JANIS: That's right. *(Beat)* I'm not quite sure how to say this. It seems someone rang up on your behalf. Well, not on your behalf. That's altogether wrong. They wanted to warn us about you.

GINA: There. You see there? It's started.

JANIS: I know. I can't understand it. *(To WALTER)* Somebody rang up the council to say [...] you were a property owner.

STEPHIE: Sod it. *(To WALTER)* Is it true? Are you?

WALTER: No [...]I told you, they froze all my assets [...] my bank account.

JANIS: If it's true, you can say good-bye to a council flat.

STEPHIE: [...] and forget all about legal aid. We'll have to take this under review. If we continue to act for you, the current rate is £175 per hour, if I don't levy a surcharge for attempting to bilk us.

WALTER: But it's not true, I tell you. It's my family [...] my sister, hah? She has houses she doesn't know about [...] and she drugged our mother into thinking I was incompetent. I own nothing. She's a grasping ... gratuitous Great Dane. She resented me owning my own name, as a result I've never owned anything [...] I've been disowned, you see? The mater doesn't realize I've gone.

STEPHIE: All right, steady on. We can easily trace the deeds.

LISA: What do you say to my husband? What happens to him?

STEPHIE: He's not epileptic, is he?

JANIS: He looks positively frightful.

GINA: It's the priests, I tell you.

STEPHIE: Hold his [...] one of you [...] one of you ring 999.

LISA: What is happening to him?

STEPHIE: Think it's a stroke of some kind.

GINA: I tell you, they're working their revenge.

As they rush in to help WALTER, MINNY appears.

MINNY: What would *you* do in this situation – treat him privately, sending the bill to his family? I fancy even the most hard-hearted among us would sooner collapse ourselves than do nothing for Walter. Face it, we're hopelessly soft in many ways [...] when you think about other countries. Walter was rushed into hospital after suffering what was assessed as a mild stroke, his personal circumstances put to one side. We still treat the patient, not his bank balance.

Hospital treatment room. LISA is helping WALTER cross the room. He walks with deliberate care, as though he is consciously planning every step. His speech is post-stroke slow.

MINNY: (*Sotto voce*) It's been three days now, and they're on the point of releasing him. But there are two things worth noting here. I wonder how many can spot them [...] All right, where exactly are they going from here and who are the people in charge of the case? They're not British, are they.

JAMEELA: You don't have to rub it in.

MINNY: But isn't that very much the point?

JAMEELA: If they didn't need us, they wouldn't employ us. Or do you think it's easy to dodge people's prejudices the whole time? You're British, so how can you know? Has anyone ever said of you, Would you prefer not to be addressed by this woman? Press the red button for yes.

MINNY: Your patient's in difficulty.

WALTER: Can't […] can't catch breath.

LISA: Don't speak […] look what you doing.

WALTER: Orange curtains […] very unlucky.

LISA: I told you – floor, your feet. Never mind curtains […] and they're blue.

WALTER: I tell you orange is unlucky.

LISA: […] and I tell you they're blue. Walls are white […] no orange nowhere.

WALTER: They issued a general warning this morning – the future's orange. We're going to have to submit.

LISA: I don't know what you say. You must sit down […] get your rest. Do not talk. Do not think about nothings. I will see about tea.

WALTER: Draw back the curtains, quick.

LISA: Please stop talking nonsense. I am coming back. *(She crosses to the door to be met by JAMEELA, in hijab and trousers)*

JAMEELA: You're up and about, good. We don't encourage staying abed or even in the bedroom. The sooner the patient re-integrates, the sooner they can recover. In your husband's case […] *(To WALTER)*

LISA: How much longer, doctor?

JAMEELA: I'm only an OT, love, not a doctor. You just call me Jameela and tell me your problem. You wish to complain of your treatment, is that right? A male nurse, preferably British? Technically, that option's open to you, but in practical fact [...]

LISA: You are Muslim [...] and a woman!

JAMEELA: And your unfortunate spouse is my patient. If you're not preferenced, then nothing is wrong. We've grown used to working amidst such handicaps. Here they don't like us at all, but they need us, and so, with misgivings, they accept us ... at least until a patient is lost. My record is clean, and your husband looks to be in no danger.

WALTER: Ask her where she was trained!

JAMEELA: You see? He's taking immediate interest. Turkmenistan before serving on the Afghan front.

LISA: I am Russian!

JAMEELA: Then perhaps you consider us enemies to the knife. Please don't. My ministrations are, as they say, without frontiers.

LISA: But [...] how did you come here? How did they let you?

JAMEELA: I told you – they're desperate. My English is sometimes better than theirs [...] and I arrive, if you'll pardon me, before the flood. *(Beat)* I speak Russian, of course, but I'll address you in English, for Walter's sake. The good news is this wasn't a real stroke. Consultant's notes mention facial paralysis, but that only lasted a day and a half. *(To WALTER directly)* You've been here for nearly a week now. We're keen to get rid of you! You're too healthy!

LISA: Did you marry in England?

JAMEELA: We did, but we didn't know one another very well. Hamid was escaping the Taliban in Kandahar, and, through the underground, finished up here. We've just managed to get his sister out safely. There are some exercises we need going over. You both need to promise you'll do these at home.

LISA: *(Meant to be speaking Russian)* But we have no home at the moment. His family was awful to me, they tried to bribe me and then called me whore [...] and then finally, when they left their house [...]

JAMEELA: Wait a minute. What is she saying?

WALTER: I don't speak Russian!

LISA: They kick us out[…]stop his money.

WALTER: *(A low moan throughout)* The orange traffic cones in the street […]shaped like rockets […] set for attack.

LISA: You hear? Again orange. He thought those curtains were orange.

JAMEELA: Perhaps he's dazzled by sunlight. Two weeks in confinement. It's apt to make anyone colour-blind. Trust me, he's not mentally ill – just frustrated. But what's this you say about no money? Let Walter tell me himself.

LISA: His family were horrid to me.

JAMEELA: I don't want to hear about you for the moment […] Walter? What's this your wife says about orange? Can you explain it to me?

WALTER: You're an infidel, are you […] gone against your religion?

JAMEELA: That's not what we're here to discuss. *(She produces an orange scarf from somewhere on her person)* I want to try something.

LISA: No – what are you doing?

JAMEELA: If his right side was paralysed, we'd work exclusively on the right side […] What does this orange scarf suggest to you, Walter?

LISA: You're not going to show him your underwear!

JAMEELA: Don't be silly! *(To WALTER)* An evil portent, is that right?

WALTER: My family […] are absolute bastards.

JAMEELA: That's what your good wife was saying. That's what this scarf represents to you, does it? A breakdown of civilization. Parents don't speak to their children […] husbands sleep with their mothers-in-law. Only it has nothing to do with this scarf. It's completely mine. My husband bought it for me on our good-luck day and every day I wear it I feel specially empowered. *(Therapy)* Lift your arm […] can you do that for me? *(To LISA)* And he was disabled already, is that right?

WALTER: I was born with it – that's right. My mother thought more of the Oxford May Ball than she did about my arrival. You're not English, I notice.

JAMEELA: Do you wish to hold that against me?

WALTER: No! Against my family – they'd go apeshit. They're what's wrong with the health service. Love it.

JAMEELA: And I hate it, thank you all the same.

WALTER: My mother would have you detained, drawn and quartered.

JAMEELA: Please stop talking like this […] before I complain about *you*. *(To them both)* These are the daily exercises I've written out. Please see that he does them regularly at home.

LISA: I told you, we have no home.

JAMEELA: You're not just being metaphorical?

WALTER: They've kicked us out, disinherited me, tried to make us both vagrants under the law.

JAMEELA: *(To LISA)* This isn't a part of his orange syndrome – you really were evicted […] from somewhere?

LISA: *(No English)* Believe me, that's how it all start. He refuse to live without me, and they make scandal so we have to leave our flat.

JAMEELA: Because I'll have to be honest with you. There isn't enough wrong with you to keep you here. They need the bed. We're getting ready to send you home.

LISA: But we have no home. Are you saying he must get ready to look for work? It's not possible.

JAMEELA: Where have you been staying until now?

WALTER: Hotel Regent, until three days ago.

LISA: I told you – they ask us to leave.

JAMEELA: I can't send you off to a bench on the Common [...] I see outpatients one day per week at our house. If you could find somewhere near there [...]

LISA: We have no money.

WALTER: I could stay with you!

JAMEELA: At our house, you mean? That's not possible. My young sister-in-law has just come here, from Kandahar. Very strictly brought up.

YELENA arrives, poking her head round the door. She is meant to be speaking Russian to LISA.

WALTER: Would we have to meet?

JAMEELA: *(To LISA)* Is he seriously asking me [...]?

WALTER: I wouldn't take up much space. That park bench [...] on the Common?

JAMEELA: Let me talk to Hamid about it. *(Goes off, nearly colliding with YELENA)* Excuse me.

YELENA: Allo? I come no good place? *(Seeing LISA, meant to be speaking Russian)* Ah, no, there you are. *(Beaming to the others)* My name ... Yelena. *(With gestures)* My [...] my [...] *(Seeing WALTER, in Russian)* Oh, bunnykins! *(Crosses to embrace him)*

LISA: Control yourself [...] Mother! *(Explaining, in English)* My mama.

WALTER: How the hell did she get here?

LISA: I don't know. *(To YELENA)* Are you out of your mind? They don't know you!

YELENA: Sorry [...] *ochin* sorry. I had the most awful time finding this place.

LISA: Speak in English, for Walter's sake.

YELENA: *(Small laugh)* What the hell are you talking about?

LISA: We are sorry – only English spoken here.

WALTER: Oh, don't worry about me – talk your heads off.

LISA: *(Turning his chair to face the other way)* We will away from the nasty orange curtains.

YELENA: Is he always as helpless as this?

LISA: What do you mean? Walter's lovely.

WALTER: What's she saying – I'm ugly as sin? She can't bear to look at me, is that it? *(To YELENA)* I know how you feel, love.

YELENA: *(In front of WALTER)* Here, I brought you this money.

LISA: *(Trying to block his view)* Shh. Where did you get that?

YELENA: Does that matter? You wrote you had none.

LISA: Shh.

YELENA: You said he couldn't understand.

LISA: He can see, can't he? I don't even know how you come to be here.

YELENA: You don't have to worry about that.

LISA: How did you come in? *I'm* not even allowed to stay.

YELENA: But you're married to English, why not? Why not, Lisechka? You never tell me until it's too late, and then you fuss when I panic. Whose fault is that?

LISA: Never mind; I'm here for the moment.

YELENA: So am I.

LISA: You sold your shoe shop. Did you also let go of your flat?

YELENA: Of course not.

LISA: Sasha stole for you! Oh, Mama!

YELENA: No, none of those things.

LISA: But I'm meant to be giving you money. Take it back.

YELENA: But you need it.

LISA: Not at the price that you paid for it […] and I don't think I want you to tell me.

YELENA: I still own the flat […] Yelena Churkova is looking after the business. Looking after. It's still mine

LISA: Sasha's not in the flat, is he?

YELEVA: Why not?

LISA: It won't be there when you get back. Thugs will have smashed it up.

YELENA: Please don't talk like that.

LISA: This didn't come from him, did it – drugs money?

YELENA: Of course not.

WALTER: We don't need your pittance. She's supposed to be poor. Well, I'm not.

YELENA: What is he saying?

LISA: Exactly what I am – take it back.

YELENA: *(To WALTER)* Lisa no food […] no good husband. No food.

LISA: Don't talk that way to him.

YELENA: Well, why did you write me?

LISA: I was scared! All right? You're my mother. I never expected you to answer, let alone come

YELENA: Well, I'm here now.

LISA: And I'm even more scared. You haven't got money like this […] or the airfare.

YELENA: I got a job with a Russian in London.

LISA: I don't believe you. *I* can't get a job.

YELENA: Not a real one, all right. But a real invitation. Here, look. For six months, eh? *(Shows passport)*

LISA: You got this through Russian who lives in Great Britain.

YELENA: Half a million of them. It's called Londongrad.

LISA: I had every right to be frightened. Those are gangsters, Mama.

YELENA: Who are you to talk? A cripple without any money? Oh, yes, you did very well.

LISA: We're alive at least […] and safe. This illness of Walt's cost us nothing. And the flat we'll be moving into.

YELENA: It's not a permanent job, love of God.

LISA: What's not?

YELENA: I told you, I still have the shop and the flat […] I borrowed the money I gave you. And the man said, It's yours for a favour to a friend when you arrive.

LISA: I think I hate what this sounds like.

YELENA: Well, it's done now […] for your sake.

LISA: Oh, Mama, what have you done? You should know not to trust anything Sasha's involved in.

YELENA: A mother who can't trust her own son?

LISA: He's also a crook, always has been, everything he knows beyond home is crooked. Are you forgetting how he hit me and stole all my jewellery for drink? When we were younger, his fist was always in my face.

YELENA: Stop. No more. A mother's a pawn for her children. You left me shaking with worry. Sasha came in […] he offered help. You want me to turn him down […] turn him in? I can't do that. No mother can.

LISA: You might have come here to die. Who knows?

YELENA: Doesn't matter – my children are safe.

LISA crosses tearfully to WALTER, fussing with him to take her mind off her pain.

WALTER: What's the matter? I told her we didn't need her money.

LISA: Of course, we need it.

WALTER: And you told her I couldn't support you, is that it? I'll support you […] … support your whole family […] bring 'em on.

TAMARA, a Russian woman between YELENA'S age and LISA'S, comes on.

TAMARA: How much longer do we have to wait? *(To YELENA)* I'm not holding the car here like a taxi. We'll leave in five minutes, and you'll arrive late, taking your own consequences.

YELENA: Oh, no, I'm going with you. Don't worry. I just had to see my daughter […] you understand

LISA: I want to know where you're taking my mother.

YELENA: Lisa!

TAMARA: Are you Russian?

LISA: That's right, married to English. How does she happen to be here?

YELENA: I'm working here. *(To TAMARA)* Please don't take offence.

LISA: Exactly how is that possible? I live here and can't get a job.

TAMARA: *(After a beat)* All right, you can see for yourself.

LISA: Unfortunately, my husband is ill.

TAMARA: What the fuck are we waiting round here for? *(To YELENA)* I'll say I couldn't find you and you'll have to take what you get.

YELENA: No, don't […] I'm coming with you!

LISA: I'm coming, too […] just let me talk to my […]

YELENA follows TAMARA out.

LISA: Waltechka, I go look after Mama. For short time, only for short […] *(Kisses his face)*

WALTER: What are you doing, leaving me? Just like that?

LISA: I know, I know, don't worry. I return soon. Waltechka, *lapichka*.

WATER: Oh, don't worry! You'll find me in Potter's Field!

LISA: You look after my Waltechka for me.

JAMEELA: *(Returning)* Why? What does she mean?

WALTER: Her mama's come to the rescue.

JAMEELA: What? What are you talking about? *(Watching LISA)* It's fantastic […] she just […]

WALTER: She just left me, Jameela.

JAMEELA: Oh, don't be absurd – she can't leave you like that. We need to discuss where you're going.

WALTER: Your husband don't want me, is that it? My tight-arsed fuck-of-a-family told her they were too good for her, so she left. And you want to send me back there. They're the reason I'm here! I'll come here worse next time! All your hard work gone to waste […]

JAMEELA: Don't worry, Walter. We'll look after you.

WALTER: *(Near tears of rage)* What are *you* still doing here?

JAMEELA: You mean taking your best British jobs?

WALTER: I mean in this tight-arsed fuck-of-a-country!

JAMEELA'S home. She and WALTER are going through his regular exercises. WALTER'S face has a twisted expression.

MINNY: It may come as a shock to many of you just how many have come from abroad [...] I mean qualified people like Walter's pair ... head-hunted. And they include, of course, doctors from Afghanistan. And if we depend on them, can we really object to their presence? It's a bit like cheering your home side, filled with African players, and then saying they're not entitled to the best that this country has to offer. We certainly don't stack up very well against these people. They've given Walter – a total stranger – the run of their home. He's claimed it, almost as his territorial right.

WALTER: How long has it been now, a week?

JAMEELA: The paralysis has started to reappear. You haven't been doing the exercises. Have you taken the tablets this morning?

WALTER: Are you threatening me with my family again? They could just do with a fruit basket case.

JAMEELA: You said they're no longer your people, and your wife's coming back [...] she hasn't left you. I'm sure of it. We'll do three more turns round the room before lunch. Now come on – stand.

WALTER: Unto the men of the family belongs that share that the family leaves, part of which shall go to the wife [...]

JAMEELA: *(Astonished)* Where did that come from?

WALTER: The Quran. You have it in English translation, I notice. There's Christ all else for me to read.

They are crossing the space slowly.

JAMEELA: Watch where you're putting your feet. *(A beat)* I'm impressed and a bit astonished.

WALTER: And wed not from lewdness or debauchery but from honest maids who would share your wealth […] My Lisa's an honest maid.

JAMEELA: That's why I'm sure she's coming back for you.

WALTER: Oh, yeah? Where's my wealth? *They're* the lewd ones, my family. With their big City bonuses. And I'm like the Idiot Boy in the attic. You're bearing witness to their latest attempt to have me legally axed.

JAMEELA: You're not paying attention. You'd better not say any more. You want to give them the satisfaction of a full-blown stroke?

WALTER: Allah *akbar*.

JAMEELA: I'm sure He hears you without the words. Let's move.

Raised voices off. They stop. The more JAMEELA hears, the more preoccupied she becomes, eventually letting WALTER sit down again.

WALTER: That's your young niece, is it?

JAMEELA: Sister-in-law.

WALTER: You don't want to introduce us, is that it?

JAMEELA: I told you, she's very strict.

WALTER: I'm hardly your average alpha male, am I.

HAMID: *(Off)* You're going to take off that costume immediately.

FARIDA: *Ze zum chE le menze ka-um.* (Small 'e' as in English unstressed 'the'; large E as in 'egg'; u a bit like oo in 'book', nearer to Russian 'Hy' [nu], well?!) I'm on my way to worship.

HAMID: And you'll please to speak in English.

JAMEELA: *(Meeting them, off)* Would you both like to remember we have a guest who's recovering from a severe illness? At least keep your voices down.

WALTER: Please tell your niece I'd be most charmed to meet her.

They advance into the room, FARIDA wearing a burqa.

JAMEELA: Sister-in-law.

HAMID: *(Coming on)* Don't you think it's about time you met some Englishmen?

FARIDA: *(Following him)* Are you trying to marry me off quick? *(Looks at WALTER)* I detest your choice.

JAMEELA: Walter's already married.

WALTER: To a Russian who left me.

JAMEELA: Keep still.

WALTER: But I'm very sympathetic. *(Attempting to speak Pashtu)* Don't help me now. *Wa assal-aam. (Grins)*

FARIDA: *Musli sagi dawo kharva gii, harf mezani* [...]I said you speak like a dog that's been poisoned.

HAMID: At least he tries to communicate.

FARIDA: *(To WALTER)* I suppose they told you how they rescued me from the claws of the Taliban?

JAMEELA: I don't recall saying—

HAMID: Wasn't that the plan? We'd escape back through Russia, then send for you once we were safe.

FARIDA: You mean that was part of *your* plan.

HAMID: I'm the head of the family. You were all of 15.

FARIDA: I'm an adult now, by western standards, and you left me to fend for myself.

HAMID: We left you with female cousins who sent you to safety in Pakistan. What's the problem?

FARIDA: Is that honestly what you think happened to me?

HAMID: Are you miffed because we couldn't send for you sooner? It wouldn't matter to you if we're tortured, risking our lives the whole time [...]

FARIDA: *(Overlapping)* You want to talk about torture? Fine. Those cousins you left me with supported the council of elders. The elders had heard about you ... they knew you were Soviet trained, that you married a wife who was Soviet trained. *(To WALTER)* Our father was beheaded because of his son's connection with Russia. Did they bother to tell you that?

JAMEELA: Will you both please refrain from conducting a brawl? Our patient is still recovering. *(To HAMID)* Did you ask if there'd been any telephone calls?

HAMID: She telephoned yesterday afternoon [...]from a house in Surrey. *(Back to FARIDA)* I told you to take that ridiculous thing off.

JAMEELA: That's no reason for speaking to her like that [...]and how can you call it ridiculous?

HAMID: It's deliberate provocation. That's what's ridiculous. She intends it as a uniform.

FARIDA: If you brought me here under false pretences. *(HAMID scoffs)*

JAMEELA: Can't we talk about this as a family? *(She crosses into the room)* You haven't eaten since you arrived. Perhaps if we all sat down to a meal together, and you told us calmly—

FARIDA: – how you kidnapped me? Soviet warthog. He did this for love of *you*.

WALTER: Suppose you don't want to hear how love led *me* astray?

HAMID: So now what – I'm guilty of patricide?

WALTER: I didn't think so.

JAMEELA: Why don't we just let her tell us what happened.

HAMID: We were told you left of your own accord.

FARIDA: Because I thought I was visiting aunts in Peshawar.

HAMID: So you're visiting your brother instead. Where's the kidnap? You're out of danger.

FARIDA: I was only in it thanks to you! The council of elders absolved me of your crimes.

HAMID: They ordered our father's beheading […]

FARIDA: […]because of *your* crimes.

JAMEELA: We never attacked anybody, Farida.

FARIDA: Your Soviet troops killed one and a half million.

JAMEELA: They were never my troops, dear. I was only Soviet trained.

HAMID: What's the point of explaining it to her? *(To FARIDA) You* were never attacked, were you?

FARIDA: What do you mean? We were all targeted. Hamid Sayaf's wife is pro-Soviet. His father was beheaded by order of the local *jurga*. He finished his training in Russia. Sayaf's sister now, where is *she*? Kinder just to forget me, you know […] let me find my own life.

HAMID: So what are you saying? You're a Taliban playgirl?

JAMEELA: Hamid!

HAMID: What term of endearment did she call you?

FARIDA: One thing I'm not is an Af-English wart […]

JAMEELA: Can we stop using that word?

FARIDA: [...] someone you put into English state schools, who conforms simply to keep from being attacked. Other Asian girls tell you, 'It's all right, do like we do. English boys are all right, they're like us, educated. It's not like it is back home. Only their home is totally different than mine. Bangladesh is totally different. For them the odd coffee is different, the odd kiss, the odd roll in the haystack.

JAMEELA: Farida!

FARIDA: Don't think I don't know what goes on. If these are just stories, what about all those operations on girls to become born-again Muslims once they've travelled abroad? Are you saying they never took place [...] that you were never involved in such things? You're medical people. I don't believe you.

HAMID: And is that what all this is about? You're making a fashion statement?

FARIDA: All I wanted was safety.

HAMID: Why else did we send for you, for God's sake! I wrapped myself up in a Shadori to escape. But you're here now.

FARIDA: And *you* look ridiculous. Fashion statement.

JAMEELA: No one's saying you can't be devout. There are thousands of women right here in Hounslow. *Hamdardi ku hamdardee koo* – We sympathize.

HAMID: Does she imagine it's like a bus ride from Qalat to Kandahar? *(To FARIDA)* The asylum process is torture, you know. Months of enforced segregation [...] detention [...] little short of prison rations [...] and that's without counting attacks in the street. Shopfronts torched by racist gangs [...] workers crippled for life.

FARIDA: Why subject yourself? Why Britain?

HAMID: Where else would you put us, Guantanamo? It was only because it was Britain that we were given a proper hearing [...] our medical background was sought. But even now, with a proper leave to remain, there are problems. Constant surveillance [...] arrest and detention. Jameela was arrested and held twice in the last year.

JAMEELA: She doesn't need to know that.

HAMID: Excuse me, I think she does. *(To FARIDA)* She could have been tortured herself, for all you know.

JAMEELA: But it never really happened.

FARIDA: And what of my trouble? When did you think about that?

HAMID: I told you—

FARIDA: Two years too late. First I tried to hide my identity […] moving villages […] seeking out cousins who'd pass me off as a neighbour whose family were killed. But then one of them said she could no longer live with deception. One elder bribed her. I was betrayed. Can't you imagine what happened next?

JAMEELA: Are you telling us *you* were tortured?

FARIDA: I'm still alive.

HAMID: You mean it was worse? You already need to be born-again, is that it? My teenage sister, the dancing queen of Qulab Chakan. Or is it too late for hymenoplasties? We need to screen you for AIDS.

JAMEELA: Can't you see it's nothing like that?

HAMID: I can't see anything, literally. But she'll take that off before I have another word with her.

WALTER: *(After a pause)* Allah *akbar*.

JAMEELA: Walter, please shut up. You ought to know it's not helping.

WALTER: But I happen to think she's right.

HAMID: *(As he leaves)* You might remind our guest he invited himself here and we can easily put him out.

WALTER: I agree with you, love. Death to the corporation.

JAMEELA: Believe me, this is more than a student protest. Hamid believes they've been targeting us. *(Going off)* Honestly, she doesn't understand the situation.

WALTER: Which one of us leaves the room?

FARIDA: What did my brother mean, you invited yourself?

WALTER: I'm their patient [...] I had a stroke. *(Starts to move)* I'll get out of your way.

FARDIA: Why do you follow the Quran? Are you just making fun of us?

WALTER: I mean it – I think you're right.

FARIDA: But it is not your business.

WALTER: Right. *(She moves to help him)* What you think you're doing?

FARIDA: The Quran bids us to help the enfeebled. Never trust them with money, but do what you can to assist them.

WALTER: I'm not [...]

FARIDA: *(Assisting him to sit)* Please do not speak. You must allow me to help you relax.

WALTER: Suppose you wouldn't like to hear how I got like this.

FARIDA: If it does not involve giving you my money.

WALTER: My family dishonoured my wife.

FARIDA: And mine will most probably force me to marry.

WALTER: They told her she wasn't good enough for them and then proved it by turning her criminal.

FARIDA: I was told I'd find sanctuary at a refugee camp in Peshawar. Then I was told I was singled out for transport to the West from Islamabad. What's that? I said. Sex traffic? Oh, no, they said. Your family have sent for you. My family are patricides. How does that make me safe?

WALTER: Death to infidel families.

FARIDA: May they be wart-ridden anyway.

WALTER: You don't know where I can get hold of Semtex.

MINNY: *(Stepping into the action)* I'll be perfectly honest, I wasn't really expecting that. These people keep to themselves – the women especially. And while I have been invited to attend Muslim prayer sessions with women, they made me feel such an outsider that [...] Well, I won't really go into that. But this business of the sister helping Walter is a complete shock to me [...] I'm sure it's significant. I just can't see how, at the moment. Nor, to be honest, am I completely genned up about this next scene, the Russian business. I mean I know there's a translation of sorts. I can follow that closely enough. But the precise details [...] Well, see what you make of them. There's a Russian entrepreneur, who's placed himself in exile, here in England, in Surrey, no less, and he claims to be an enemy of the present Russian government, which we all assume to be as undemocratic as Russian governments always have been. And he claims the KGB are out to get him [...] made several attempts on his life. But now he's offered to help Lisa and her mother [...]

LISA and YELENA are in a big salon in a big house in Surrey.

LISA is at the window. They are meant to be speaking Russian.

YELENA: Can you get a good look at his face?

LISA: He's not a football club owner anyway.

YELENA: What?

LISA: No! I don't see him! There's the driver and that ... his personal assistant. She spotted me. Looks like she's heading this way.

YELENA: Are we their prisoners or what?

LISA: How do *I* know? You say he engaged *you,*

YELENA: She told me he did. Don't blame *me. I* didn't put us in here. *(To TAMARA as she enters)* Are you keeping us here as your prisoners?

TAMARA: Good morning. Why? Didn't you sleep well? You've eaten well at our expense […] and you call that prison. You must live lavishly. I'll have to visit you some time.

LISA: But never one word why we're here.

TAMARA: I told you before you arrived.

YELENA: You said I was doing a job for you […] what job? I've done nothing. We've hardly seen anyone.

TAMARA: *(Looking at LISA)* Who is this person again?

YELENA: I told you, this is my daughter, Lisa.

TAMARA: Very interesting. *(To LISA)* Stand over there, please.

LISA: I think you're playing with us.

TAMARA: Your mother told colleagues of ours in Moscow you could help us.

YELENA: But I never—

LISA: I don't see how that's possible.

YELENA: *(To LISA)* I said how we both might be able to help.

LISA: *(To TAMARA)* I don't think so, you see. We're from a very small village, indeed. What possible use could either of us be to people like you?

TAMARA: You don't seem to see. She's placed herself in our debt.

LISA: I don't see how she even knows you!

TAMARA: Don't be alarmed. I work with one of the richest men in England. You're privileged that he even knows your name.

LISA: You still haven't told me […]

TAMARA: No English is rich by comparison.

LISA: I don't think we want to take the chance, thank you.

TAMARA: Ask your mother to tell you. Ask her if she wants to take the consequences.

LISA: That sounds more like a threat than a privilege.

TAMARA: It's more of a missed opportunity.

LISA: I'll pay you the price of her ticket. We want to leave here as soon as possible.

TAMARA: The debt goes far deeper than that. There's her son, not to mention her daughter *(To LISA)* You've outstayed your visa.

BOGDAN BUBENOV comes on brusquely.

BUBENOV: Have you been getting acquainted with the place? The agents told me this was George Harrison's. I asked what house did he take instead. They told me I'm thinking of the drummer. They also said my property goes into the next county. I think I prefer to believe that. You can verify that. Did you go for a drive in the Maybach?

LISA: We haven't been out of this house!

TAMARA: I thought it best to wait for your return.

BUBENOV: All right, but these *are* the right people? *(To LISA)* You were well treated.

LISA: If near-kidnap is treating us well…

YELENA: *(Overlapping)* […] brilliantly, thank you. We couldn't have asked for more.

TAMARA: I was only following procedure.

BUBENOV: Fuck off *(Lightly)* All Russian women are mothers, eh? A recent attempt on my life, and she thinks there's a sniper lurking in every crevice.

TAMARA: When you never keep to a timetable, that's right.

BUBENOV: That's how I keep one step ahead of a bullet.

TAMARA: And we all suffer.

BUBENOV: All right, you can go. The ladies forgive you their barbarous treatment, and I'm not going to sack you *this* week.

LISA: And we're free to go?

TAMARA: *(Leaving)* I told them they wouldn't want to.

BUBENOV: Well, I certainly hope not […]You've heard about my breath-taking diamond collection, haven't you? You can't leave without seeing the Moussaieff Red. *(Preparing to show it to them)*

LISA: Couldn't we get this over with first? We've been here three days.

BUBENOV: You're a ballsy young woman, aren't you […] the thought you may never get home alive doesn't frighten you, does it. No, I like that, believe me. It's one sure guarantee that you will.

YELENA: Bogdan…

BUBENOV: […] Vasilich […] And your name is […]?

YELENA: What's really happened to my son? You're right – we're all mothers. I've been nearly out of my mind.

BUBENOV: Then calm yourself, Mother. Your son is all right.

LISA: He's the reason we're here, though, isn't he?

BUBENOV: What, you think I'm holding him against his will? This is Bubenov you're talking to! What could I want with your son? You ought to keep him home nights though, I'm telling you. Idiot starts screaming his head off, right before getting his throat cut. It's lucky he screamed out in my direction.

LISA: What are you talking about?

BUBENOV: He starts mouthing off in a bar he's got a beautiful sister in London, and before he's even finished the sentence, the goons start closing in. Fortunately, an associate of mine overheard him as well.

LISA: Uh-huh […] and kidnapped him.

YELENA: Lisa!

BUBENOV: Out of interest, how did *you* happen to get here? Who did you have to bribe for how much? I've been the kid's guardian angel. You can talk to him right now. But as you're asking him has he still got his teeth and are his limbs still intact, see what he says about the night we found him […] how near he came to losing it. If he doesn't break down in tears, I'll get Tamara to give you a ride home right now.

LISA: But she said we're in your debt. What's that about?

BUBENOV: I just told you.

LISA: We work for you for how long […] and doing what, exactly?

BUBENOV: It's nothing to do with a debt. I told you that, too. What use have I got for a kid that shits himself? But my colleague heard London, thought of me, and thought you and I might at least meet. Your mother thought so as well.

YELENA: I was offered a ticket […] you said you were desperate.

LISA: We've been all through this. *(To BUBENOV)* What would harming us solve? My brother deserves prison. In one sense he's better off dead. The same goes for me at the moment. My mother, as you can see, she's helpless.

BUBENOV: I'm not going to punish you really. The worst that can happen to any of you is we find that we can't do business, and you leave here the same as you came. But I don't think even that's very likely. I'm quite sure we *can* do business.

LISA: What can *we* do for someone like *you*?

BUBENOV: Your husband's people are captains of British industry.

LISA: But they've disowned him, because of me.

BUBENOV: But what if you were to tell them that you, too, were connected […] that you could open up Russian markets to them? Care to look at the Red now?

LISA: *(After a pause)* But this is storybook […] I refuse to believe it.

BUBENOV: Did you believe your marriage?

LISA: I honestly didn't know about his family. And when I found out, I didn't believe it. And now it turns out […]

BUBENOV: […]It's true, after all. It *is* a storybook. Zolushka marries her prince.

LISA: Excuse me, I've got to […]

YELENA: Oh, why do you always think the worst of everything? *I* knew, as soon as you said he was English, everything would be fine

LISA: It's not fine, though, is it. Walter's disabled, we haven't got a house, and […]

BUBENOV: And I stand here telling you everything's fine. You're perfectly right to be cautious. I would. You want to know, for a start, why I'd need your husband's, a cripple's, help. I am Russian. To the British, that's like being a cripple. We kill our neighbours, cheat our partners, we're the scourge of the world. But we've money, and they haven't, and in this particular climate, old-world scruples and prejudices vanish. Mention my name, and privileged markets open up before their eyes. Just see for yourself. *And I need their business.* I've been after it for years […] I need you, in the immediate term, to take a message to a Russian colleague.

LISA: What?

BUBENOV: I'm sure he's a KGB agent, sent from Moscow, to discredit me. I want you to meet with him.

LISA: And get myself murdered? No, thanks!

YELENA: Oh, for God's sake, Lisa.

LISA:　　　　　He talks about snipers lying in wait […]

BUBENOV:　　　That's right, and they're waiting for *me*, not a fresh, young girl from the country. What would be the point? But when he receives this message from you, who he absolutely doesn't expect, he'll know that his cover is blown, absolutely.

LISA:　　　　　And what about Walter's family?

BUBENOV:　　　They'll lick your hand. You can all move onto these grounds, if you like – your mother and Walter […]

YELENA:　　　　It's a miracle!

Something resembling a town or district square in a European setting, though it is actually a shopping precinct in an English new town. Ideally all the company are on for this, with some members stepping out of character to assume ancillary roles. These will be identified as they come up. MINNY PLAYFAIR appears first, followed, on one side, by LISA and TAMARA and, on the other, by WALTER and FARIDA and, latterly, HAMID and AUNT HENNY.

MINNY:　　　　[…] and so to this final twist. We're festively met in a burgeoning shopping precinct in one of the new towns like Telford or Milton Keynes, though it's probably closer to London than that. There are restaurants and pavement cafes and haute couture shops with more staff than clientele in them. They'll close down once the first quarter's sales come due, and then this whole area will begin to look like a giant squat. But right now it's a harbinger of hope, an oasis in the desert of downturn. All our principals are here as well. They don't all know it yet, though. Lisa's here to meet someone she's never seen.

TAMARA and LISA sit at a small pavement table. They are meant to be speaking Russian.

TAMARA:　　　Why don't you try what the French call *cassis*? It's like the Russian black currant, with rum.

MINNY:　　　　[…] and Walter thinks he's going to meet his aunt. He thinks Lisa's abandoned him, and *she* wonders if she'll ever see him again.

LISA:　　　　　Why can't I have it without?

TAMARA: You're strange for your age and circumstance. The clothes you wear – they're like the last Soviet items in stock. My granny might even choose better.

LISA: English girls dress like tarts […] and they'll die of arthritis at 30.

TAMARA: Oh, don't lecture. How would you say I dress?

LISA: No, I wasn't referring to *you*. You're fine.

TAMARA: Well, then shut up about it. I've been here far longer than you have, and I can't do anything to change local taste.

LISA: I was just talking till he gets here.

TAMARA: Yes, but why? Do you think we're ever going to be friends?

LISA: I don't know!

TAMARA: Do you know what you're meant to be doing at least?

LISA: No! […] Have a drink with him, you said.

TAMARA: And make sure you give him this envelope. *(Passes it to her)*

LISA: Do you really want me to drink alcohol?

TAMARA: Oh, for God's sake. Have what he has, if you can't think for yourself. He'll probably ask you – he's become British nice.

LISA: Well, then why aren't *you* drinking with him?

TAMARA: Haven't you worked that one out yet? I'm *not* nice. Seeing me is like seeing Bubenov, and he doesn't trust either of us.

LISA: But what does that matter if all you want is to give him this?

TAMARA: Don't ask too many questions, all right? For your own good.

LISA: What has my good got to do with it […]if it's innocent?

TAMARA: They fell out over something – *I* don't know what. Bubenov calls this a peace offering. One look at you, and he'll know it's the truth. That's all there is to it.

LISA: Nothing is ever that simple with Russians. I had the brains to get out. You think I don't know? You think I don't know that every vegetable lady has diamonds from fleecing her customers?

TAMARA: All right! You want to see your family again, don't you? Just give him the envelope.

LISA: And then what?

TAMARA: You don't want to refuse and find out.

LISA: What does *that* mean […]? Come on, what does it mean – are you threatening me?

TAMARA: Nobody's forced you to sleep with them, have they? You and your mother have been treated like guests […] like British Royalty, in fact. We've asked of you nothing so far […] except this.

LISA: That's exactly what worries me. Why?

TARAMA: I tell you, *I* don't know much […] for the same reason.

LISA: I feel like I've abandoned my husband.

TAMARA: That's how it works. All right, you want us to talk like we're friends. *I* was a vegetable lady, you know? And Bubenov helped out *my* husband, like yours. And I thought working for him would be diamond studded.

LISA: And it wasn't? He threatened to kill him if you didn't do what he said?

TAMARA: No, he'd make sure my husband killed me. We've been separated for over two years, and Bubenov would let it be known that I'm responsible for every piece of shit Sergei got in his face. He'd believe it, and my life would be over. Your husband – I've seen him – could never do that to you.

LISA: There's my husband.

TAMARA: I tell you – he's harmless. You're in the clear. Bubenov only hurts those he thinks can hurt him. Like me, like my shit-of-a-husband. Or Voronin. You keep it that way.

LISA looks round anxiously. Presently WALTER comes on with FARIDA, in burqa. WALTER'S dressed in a scaled-down version.

LISA: *(Astonished)* Walter […]? What's he doing here […] and who is *she*?

TAMARA: What the hell are you doing? He's not the one.

LISA: Why did you bring him here?

TAMARA: I don't even know who you're talking about.

LISA: Over there! He's my husband.

TAMARA: For fuck's sake. *(Standing)* Don't fuck this up […] I'm telling you. *(Leaving)* I'll collect you when he goes.

LISA: *(crossing over)* Waltechka, what are you doing here?

WALTER: Let those who commit lewdness after marriage be banished forever. My name is Abdul Jazeel.

LISA: I don't understand what you're saying.

FARIDA: Can't you see this man is afflicted?

WALTER: I'll talk to her […] for a few minutes.

LISA: Few minutes for what? Is this a joke?

WALTER: Is it? *You* tell *me*. You left me to fend for myself.

LISA: Because I did not know what would happen. But it's all right now. Mama's paid back the debt, and I'm to remain […] no visas, no police visits. I can even visit your family in peace. They'll even welcome me now […] just what we want.

WALTER: I have no more family. They turned their back on me …

LISA: I know that, but […]

WALTER: […] so I spit on them and all their material sin.

LISA: What's *happened* to you?

AUNT HENNY approaches – quite as she was before.

AUNT HENNY: Walter? It's Aunt Henny, dear. Thank you for agreeing to meet me. *(Seeing LISA)* Oh, and this must be […]

LISA: My name is Lisa […] I'm Walter's wife.

AUNT HENNY: We didn't meet formally the first time. I don't know that that's really my fault.

FARIDA: Well, it's your fault now. You've both got to leave him alone. He's experienced the worst kind of shock.

AUNT HENNY: And who is this individual?

FARIDA: I'm his carer, if it's any of your concern.

WALTER: *(Of AUNT HENNY)* She's part of the feral lot that left me like this. *(To AUNT HENNY)* And *she's* well beyond your reach.

FARIDA: You see there? You're answered. Now go away.

AUNT HENNY: It wasn't me, dear. That's what I've come here to say […]to prove to you.

LISA: But none of that matters now.

FARIDA: She's right about that.

AUNT HENNY: Will both of you leave us, please? I'm Walter's favourite aunt.

LISA: And I'm his only wife.

FARIDA: I'm his carer […] and I tell you all you must leave.

VORONIN appears. Maybe TAMARA, hidden, signals to LISA in a threatening manner. HAMID now comes on as well.

LISA: *(Seeing VORONIN approach)* Yes, I have a short meeting myself.

AUNT HENNY: I promise this won't take long.

HAMID: *(To FARIDA)* Just what do you think you're playing at?

FARIDA: I'm trying to get you in trouble, of course.

HAMID: Shut up. You know, of course, Jameela was arrested after you left.

FARIDA: She's been arrested before.

HAMID: I'm not suggesting you wanted it, but you see now why we have to be careful […] we daren't raise our heads above the parapet. Police say she's part of a heroin ring […] of all the ridiculous nonsense. They don't bother to check what we do in the health service. If we work there, we must supply drugs. Who's going to believe that we *don't*? It's worse than having a patient die. Our flat goes on the list. What do you mean, physio outpatients? These are addicts who come to your door. Police come pretending they're addicts! And the result?

FARIDA: His aunt is here to collect him.

HAMID: Have you been listening to me? They're probably conducting a search at the moment. Your personal effects – pamphlets, letters, religious texts. This is worse than saying we murdered a patient. If they succeed in holding her overnight, she'll most likely lose her job. I don't, again, say you wanted it, but you need to be clear about our position here.

The focus now is split between WALTER and AUNT HENNY at one table, LISA and VORONIN at another and FARIDA and HAMID at a third. The duologues overlap, but they are written discretely.

VORONIN: You're not the one I'm meant to meet?

LISA: Alexey Igorovich? Lisa […] Nikolayevna. Hallo.

VORONIN: Your boss sent you? I expected he'd come himself. *(Looks her over)* I don't want to be photographed with a whore. If that's his game, then forget it.

LISA: Oh, I don't think it is. Honestly, I told him I wouldn't work for him under those conditions. You know, if I had to sleep with anyone. Because I know. Secretaries in Moscow, they're all asked that question before they start. And for some of them it's okay, I guess. I mean, they all know so it must be all right.

VORONIN: But not for you.

LISA: Well, I've never worked in Moscow. But I said I wouldn't here and … I haven't had to. Everything's been fine. But look, if you're still nervous about it, I can give you the envelope now. That's all I was meant to do.

VORONIN: You don't want a drink?

LISA: No. Well, yes, that's what I'd planned, but […] it's not necessary.

They are now at the table.

VORONIN: Blackcurrant?

LISA: Yes, that is exactly what I'd like. Without anything else.

VORONIN: Naturally.

LISA: Thank you very much! *(Hands him the envelope)* Well, here you are.

They sit down.

VORONIN: I have a daughter about your age. She's a bio-technician in Smalensk […] that's a reasonable distance from Moscow.

LISA: So am I. I'm an accountant […] from Yaroslavl.

VORONIN: What the hell was he doing in Yaroslavl?

LISA: Oh, he wasn't. I'm married to English. We met here. My husband and I needed a bit more, so some Russian friends here sent me there […] I mean his office.

VORONIN: And now you find yourself sitting with me.

LISA: It's not nearly as bad as I thought it would be! I mean […] I don't mean that as bad as it sounds.

VORONIN: He said I was some sort of underworld type, is that it?

LISA: No, he didn't at all.

VORONIN: Don't you wonder why you were brought in?

LISA: What? Oh, that. That has to do with my husband's company.

VORONIN: I've nothing to do with his company. I don't know your husband.

LISA: No, this is something extra, he said. But he's anxious to do business with them. They're a big British firm, and he wants—

VORONIN: *(Overlapping)* He wants to exert undue influence. That's what it is – over everything. This government gave him asylum … and now he tells them what do to in Iraq.

LISA: *(Laughs) He* tells them?

VORONIN: He gives them the money. His money helps the campaigns in Georgia and the Ukraine. And he's personally involved in reducing the debt crisis.

LISA: Well, that's all to the good then, isn't it?

VORONIN: You really think so?

LISA: Well, he's promised to help my family and me, and we can't afford not to believe him.

VORONIN: He's a crook […] or shouldn't I tell you?

LISA: But perhaps not a killer?

VORONIN: *(Pointing)* You see those security cameras? He's hoping they'll show me accepting a bribe from a pretty young thing.

LISA: Young thing […] you mean me?

VORONIN: He's counting on it stopping me from grassing on him.

LISA: But then what happens to me? I've done nothing.

VORONIN: Are you joking? I've done even less.

LISA: But you work with him.

VORONIN: You occupy his bed. He thinks I've been after him for months.

LISA: Well, then, please tell whoever you work for I'm innocent. I'll quickly destroy the envelope. We'll pretend you received it. Please – let me go!

VORONIN: *(Opening envelope)* How much do you think he's paying me this time? He calls it investment dividends so that we both seem legit.

At which point there is a moderate explosion off but near the spot where LISA and VORONIN were standing initially. Police now close in on all three tables.

VORONIN You bitch! You meant that for me. *That's* what you were sent here to do. *(To POLICE OFFICER)* She could leave here quickly enough.

LISA: But I do nothing wrong!

Overlapping at the other table.

AUNT HENNY: Don't say a thing – I know all about it. What I mean is, you don't have to tell me your side. That's what I think I know fairly well. And I'm even better informed now that I've seen your wife. And yes, I can see how it happened clear enough. I've always said to your mother, You may think you have Walter accounted for. But he's going to surprise you one day soon, and not in ways that you can predict or easily guard against, like the money he lost. You should have seen that coming anyway, I told her. You didn't want to join the brood, I don't know why they made you. I heard her at the time, of course. She said either that or she'd lock you away in a chamber somewhere. But you're not backward. Who's going to take you? She ought to have paid for a scholarship somewhere. You could have studied an instrument or become a patron, if you couldn't play. That would have suited you down to the ground. But now they're faced with something they absolutely don't want, didn't expect and don't know what in the stratosphere to do about. *(A beat)* You're not talking. Are you taking this in?

WALTER: They want you to get me to go home.

AUNT HENNY: No – that's *not* what I'm saying at all. They know better than to try that with me. Your mother does. She's honestly worried about you, and she asked me, particularly, to find out how you are. That makes sense to you, doesn't it? And now I've seen you ... and your wife, I can honestly make my report. In your favour, don't worry. You're very happy, you're being well looked after [...]

WALTER: My wife's a whore.

AUNT HENNY: [...] you obviously want for very little indeed. *(Stops)* What? Did you say something?

WALTER: For those women who are guilty of lewdness, confine them to the house until death, unless they seek out Allah's forgiveness. And she hasn't yet, has she.

AUNT HENNY: Hasn't what? What are you talking about?

WALTER: She has no intention of doing anything like that [...] Doesn't know what it means.

AUNT HENNY: If you and your wife are having some kind of spat, all right, I'll make myself scarce. I could see she was anxious to speak with you.

WALTER: She wants my forgiveness! And those who when they do evil remember Allah and implore forgiveness only from him, they alone shall be forgiven. Only Allah can forgive.

AUNT HENNY: Good lord. Is this you? I mean, is this what you really believe?

WALTER: I cried out to her in pain [...]

AUNT HENNY: Well, yes, I know. That's why you got married.

WALTER: I was in a dark tunnel [...] nowhere to turn.

AUNT HENNY: What would you like me to do, dear? Name it. Money. I can get Prudence to give you the money she owes you, without strings. You can place a deposit on the flat you were wanting to buy. In fact, it's yours. I can guarantee purchase on my own. I don't know why you didn't come to me in the first place.

WALTER: And devour not your property in vanity […] or devour the property of others for your own wanton gain.

AUNT HENNY: I don't know what the hell you're saying. Only stop it. You're talking in tongues.

WALTER: My name is Abdul Jazeel.

AUNT HENNY: I don't care what you think you're called. I'll call you crazy in a minute […] arrange to have you sectioned or worse. You'll no doubt want to issue me with a curse or something terrible like that. And all I've ever tried to be is kind. When I nursed you all night long through the croup […] or when I told them all, last week, not to bully you. And here you are, for all the world, trying to bully *me*. It's unworthy of you, *Abdul Jazeel*. I may well be the only friend you've got.

WALTER: A kind word with forgiveness is better than almsgiving. Thank you very much, Aunt Henny.

AUNT HENNY: Oh. Well, you're very welcome, I'm sure. *(A beat)* Are you warm enough […] got everything you want to eat?

WALTER: Everything's just fine, believe me.

AUNT HENNY: I knew it must be. I mean, I knew in my bones you couldn't possibly be dead.

WALTER: No. You wouldn't care to pass on a message from me, would you?

AUNT HENNY: I'm not sure the dust has settled yet. What? What's the message?

WALTER: Trade is just like usury, and the Good Lord blighteth usury; therefore […]

AUNT HENNY: Good Lord, he's been born again!

This is the point in their conversation at which the explosion goes off. Police converge on WALTER and HAMID as well.

POLICE
DETECTIVE: That's right, lads, seize hold of him. Don't let him go. One or two of you others go in and search the place. Sounds like it came from the kitchen area … Then you'd better supervise evacuation. All you people inside there. Stay where you are. Don't attempt to exit the premises till we can lead you. The worst thing anyone can do is panic. *(Into his mobile)* That's right. I want the bomb disposal unit as quick as you like to Rudolpho's Ristorante in the Precinct.

AUNT HENNY: Oh, but this is outrageous. This boy's done nothing at all. We have been sitting here the whole time. The explosion was all the way in there. Apart from all that, my nephew happens to be seriously handicapped. You'd have better luck looking for someone without arms.

HAMID: You know you can't charge us with anything. Search. My wife and I are medical experts […] employed by the British Government. I sometimes work as Home Office pathologist.

VORONIN: This woman just tried to assassinate me!

General mayhem superseded by the commanding appearance of MINNY PLAYFAIR, stepping up and addressing the audience directly.

MINNY: All right, I'm going to suspend the action since we've arrived at what I consider the critical point […] or rather move it forward. Three people have been arrested for the incident that took place a moment ago […] and we can assume that at least one of them will be charged. The public inquiry element of this case begins now as I invite all to comment […] or apportion blame.

PRUDENCE: *(Stepping forward)* You mean on the mother, I know. It's always the mother's fault.

MINNY: Not at all. No one's been charged yet.

PRUDENCE: Why not? In cases like this, I'm here to be pilloried. He's hideously deformed, and I'm not a self-sacrificing drone, with my hand out for charity, so it's all my fault.

MINNY: But what about the so-called Afghan connection?

AUNT HENNY: I don't for a minute believe there is one.

PRUDENCE: Well, what do *you* know? They get hold of him in the reduced Health Service, then indoctrinate him. It's obvious. Music therapy. My sister's an absolute henny.

AUNT HENNY: What I actually said was […]

LOVEDAY: I'd like to say something first, if I may […]

JANIS: Just who do you think you are?

MINNY: Everybody's going to be given all the space they need. That's what […]

LOVEDAY: I'd like to say in support of my mother […]

PRUDENCE: I never asked you either. Stay well clear, Loveday.

JANIS: With a name like that […]

LOVEDAY: Most of my life I've lived in the shadowed fact of my brother […] how much luckier I was than him, how I had to make up for the things he couldn't do. And now he may well be a criminal, so what does that say about me? I cleaned up once before after he did something *questionable*. I didn't want him to make the same mistake twice. I thought of myself first, all right. But who wouldn't, in my place? And I didn't ask to be put in my place. I reacted to circumstances, just like everybody. Is that all right with everybody?

JANIS: Just a second. You must be […] Are *you* the one that planted that news about your brother? It must be you.

LOVEDAY: I beg your pardon?

JANIS: The phone call I got saying he was a property owner and wasn't entitled to council accommodation.

LOVEDAY: You must be dreaming, dear.

JANIS: Ah-huh. Hearing you just now, the jealousy […] It's as blatant as a traffic bollard.

LOVEDAY: How do you know? All of you. You've never been in my place.

JANIS: Not sure I want to be: *Loveday*. Think I'd change my name by deed poll, for a start. Not sure I wouldn't rather be called Deed Poll.

STEWART: *(Stepping forward)* I think the evidence is conclusively against Walter.

PRUDENCE: Et tu, Stewart? That's very encouraging.

LOVEDAY: That's hideously unfair.

PRUDENCE: Attack Walter and you attack your wife's mother […] a major shareholder in your own company.

STEWART: And Walter resigned, didn't he.

PRUDENCE: Because *you* forced him out. I told you I couldn't allow him to leave.

STEWART: But that's the incriminating motive for this.

PRUDENCE: What?

STEWART: *We* own this shopping precinct. We just acquired it in the last quarter […] from Weatherborough Council. They were leery about having to raise property taxes again in the clamour for more council housing, so we were able to pick it up relatively cheap.

PRUDENCE: And you're saying my son, who can't read a balance sheet right side up, was able to intercept the sale?

STEWART: No! I'm saying that's why he could have planted the bomb […] harmless as it turned out to be.

PRUDENCE: *He's* harmless. He didn't even know about the sale.

STEWART: He knew enough about our holdings to offer the stock as collateral for buying a flat.

PRUDENCE: Balderdash. No, just plain balls. Loveday, please keep your husband in check.

LOVEDAY: He's making complete sense.

STEWART: I've already been questioned as a material witness.

PRUDENCE: You've already fingered my son!

STEWART: The facts speak for themselves.

LOVEDAY: It's a matter of public record, public weal.

PRUDENCE: And if I instigate a boardroom coup [...]

LOVEDAY: What the hell for?

STEWART: I take no pleasure in this, Prudence.

PRUDENCE: I think we'll ensure you take no profit as well.

BETTY: *(Stepping forward) I'd* like to ask a quick question, if I may.

MINNY: Is it relevant?

BETTY: It's related, I think, very much so.

MINNY: Your name is [...]?

BETTY: Betty Thomas. From Great Yarmouth. I came over here with my husband Ben.

MINNY: And you came here because of the case [...] because of all the publicity [...]

BETTY: No, nothing to do with that, I *wish*. I didn't even know about it until this afternoon [...] and then I wished I hadn't heard.

MINNY: That's intriguing – why?

BETTY: We had our digital clamped.

MINNY: I'm not with you.

BETTY: Clamped […] you know, confiscated. Our digital camera!

MINNY: Oh, because you wanted to take a photo of the scene. But surely you can understand. They've been besieged since it happened.

BETTY: No, I never even thought about it. First I thought they were trying to give my husband a hand. He's an invalid, you see, in a chair. But no […] turns out *he's* the problem. This waitress come out, instead of taking our order, she says she can't serve us. I thought, Oy, this is discrimination. Sod it, who wants to go to Strasbourg over a flipping cup of tea? But then the manager comes out, and he says he needs to have a look at our digital, would you believe? Oh, and by the way, they can't accommodate us. I thought, then, That's a bloody cheek and no mistake. Soon as he gives us the digital, I'm out of the district and all. Hallo, Southend-on-Sea, he's going to take that attitude. But no, seems he's in a right strop and all. We have to wait while he rings the authorities. And that's when the 20 pence dropped […] about this terrorist thing.

MINNY: You took a photo, and he thought […]

BETTY: Sod the photo […] and the camera at this point. What I want to ask is if his corporation owns the precinct, can we recover the damages?

STEWART: What, the loss of your camera? Of course not.

BETTY: I told you I'm no longer bothered by that. But we were nearly arrested, you know […] our good name smudged. Never put a foot wrong, either of us. Even kept our tax disk up to date […]

STEWART: And you weren't arrested, were you? Let alone charged.

BETTY: We were *persona non grata*.

STEWART: And what is that, speaking in relative terms? We've been landed with a white fucking elephant. Shops are dropping like nine pins anyway. Or maybe you think this adds local colour. We might as well talk about poisonous mains underneath.

BETTY: I dunno what you're on about, I'm sure. All I'm saying is if you own the pavement here beneath our feet, how much are you liable for what takes place?

STEPHIE: It's a fair point. Remember me? I'm the solicitor.

STEWART: And you can tell her we're not liable at all.

STEPHIE: I wasn't suggesting you are, but this whole business, you're saying, comes down to a family feud? It's taking things to extremes, don't you think?

STEWART: His own sister says he ought to be locked up.

HAMID: And what about us, the Afghan community? We'll be the first and the hardest to suffer. Muggings, mosques set on fire. Did *we* put him up to it? *(Including the women in his reference)* They're all saying *you* did.

GINA: I'm saying it's all down to voodoo. *(To BETTY)* You've got to come with me, dear, out of this morass.

BETTY: I dunno what you think you're doing.

GINA: I'm telling you, aren't I? *They* cast a spell on me. Her and that husband of hers took up in my house, and I asked them to leave, and so *she* cast a revenge spell on me. My house was condemned … my sister-in-law died of cancer […] and then my husband was banged up inside. And he never even took Paracetamol.

BETTY: And how exactly is that my concern?

GINA: Exactly when was your husband struck down with affliction?

BETTY: Is that any of your business?

GINA: You were making it public a minute ago.

BETTY: I was asking what right he thought he had—

GINA: It's got worse in the last two months, hasn't it. He could walk a bit with sticks […] and now he can't.

BETTY: And now he can't.

GINA: You have a job helping him to the toilet, in fact.

BETTY: That's right. He spends his days messing himself. Charming, eh? For a man that photograph shops used to pay to display in their windows. Now we're lucky if his photo ain't featured on *Crimewatch*.

Crowd noises focussed on WALTER directs her attention there, and she crosses to him.

BETTY: And you're the one that'd done that to us … only you. You give the disabled an even worse name. *(To PRUDENCE)* Do us all wonders if he topped himself, your son.

PRUDENCE: Are you asking me to persuade him?

JANIS: This isn't a practical joke. I'll be known for helping the Wheelchair Terrorist. They'll ask for my cards by the end of the week.

FARIDA: At least you could have done it with some expertise. Now we're all under suspicion for nothing.

HAMID: This is not why we brought you to England.

FARIDA: He's *your* patient, for pity's sake. All we did was went for a walk.

HAMID: Are you saying he's *not* guilty – you did it, after all?

FARIDA: Of course not. I'd have done damage.

HAMID: Will you keep your voice down?

VORONIN has TAMARA in tow.

VORONIN: How can you dare to deny it? I saw you conferring together […] just before you came to meet me. What was that but a coordinated attack?

LISA: But the explosion was way over there. *(To TAMARA)* Nothing's going to happen to my mother, is it?

TAMARA: You mean you want me to lie like the English? Lapichka, I don't know.

LISA: But this is nothing like what happened with your husband, is it? You told me—

TAMARA: Bubenov would make sure my husband killed me. I said your husband could never kill you in the same way.

VORONIN: Police are now saying he tried to kill me. But he failed, and Bubenov doesn't like his hitmen to miss.

LISA: He'll kill my mama. *(Moving precipitously towards WALTER)* Oh, Waltechka, you've got to tell them it is not true.

TAMARA: They're getting ready to charge, for God's sake. Don't volunteer.

VORONIN: Why not? She'll make a clean breast of it.

LISA: He done nothing, officer. Officer?

MINNY: I think Tamara is right, in a way. The best thing everybody can do at the moment is leave it all to the people in charge. They're hardly going to torture Walter, are they?

WALTER: Why not? You don't think my efforts are worth it, is that it? The cripple's worth only a caution because he missed?

MINNY: This is one time that you can be thankful for your condition.

WALTER: Are you sure about that? This isn't the Special Olympics of Terrorism. You can't sort us like you'd sort out the under-fives. Several lifetimes have gone into this. Several civilizations. Let me beg you all to be ready for it, because some time, sooner than you know, we're not going to miss. You should have killed us when you had the chance.

Final fade.

Pin spot on WALTER.

Fete

Performed by Exeter University Drama students, under the direction of Martin Harvey, on 23 March 2010.

SHEILA	Louise Beck
ZHENIA	Sarah Elghady
TOMASSINA (TOMI)	Abigail Evans
HANNAH	Rebekah Peake
COURTNEY	Georgina Bennett
CYRIL	Matthew Harris
CHARLOTTE	Charlotte Howitt
CHLOE	Olivia Clements
ISLA	Chioma Anyanwu
KACEY	Jennifer Scourfield
GRACE DAVID	Catrin Sheridan
GALYA	Katie Bobroff
IRINA	Felicia Rogers
MARK	George Vafakis
FERN	Holly Clark
CHARLES PENGE	Daniel Barron
CALEB	Charles O'Reardon
WILLIAM CRUMB	Matthew Williams

Church of England school somewhere in provincial England

Early morning in spring. The event takes place in a field alongside the school grounds under an oblong marquee that resembles a marketplace. SHEILA, in charge of the fete committee, is the first to arrive. She is diffident in her movements and seems to be looking for someone. She also refers to her computer plan of the arrangements for the afternoon. And there is a pile of rubbish not immediately apparent. Much of the action overlaps as more characters come on.

SHEILA: *(To herself)* Oh, lord, that looks ominous. I'd better [...] *(Gets out her mobile and punches a number)* Hallo, I'd like to [...] Oh, yes. *(Listens)* Twenty percent chance precipitation [...] Ten percent heavy showers ... three per cent thunderstorm? But how can that be? This is England, not the Costa del Storm Warning. We're the first week of April. *(On the mobile)* Hallo, Charlotte? It's me, I'm [...] Sheila, yes [...] at the site. But there's no one else yet. Feels like I'm committing an early-morning break-in – there's no [...] Cyril Learmouth, who's he? I thought Raymond Tong was the groundsman in charge [...] Oh, lord. Well, it can't be helped, only now I have to chase after [...] someone else. And the weather report's none too promising. I just checked. I presume the Central Met Office, whatever it's called. The automated message thing-y. She said chance of thunder [...] Oh, yes, do get here as soon as you can. I feel we should face this together. *(Listens)* Well, no, it's not an ordeal, exactly. I'm not awake yet. *(Sees the rubbish)* Oh, good Lord above. No, I promise you nothing at all. You don't even have to – Oh – h [...] *(As an expletive) femme fatale.* *(Calling)* Cyril? Mr Learmouth?

ZHENIA and her friend TOMASSINA come on, probably bearing things for the fete. ZHENIA looks too young to be the mother of school-age children, though she is exactly that age.

ZHENIA: *(Russian accent)* Good morning, Mrs Budgeon. This is my friend neighbour [...]

SHEILA: Have you seen that?

ZHENIA: What?

SHEILA: Friday-night binge brawlers left their deposits.

ZHENIA: *(Looks)* Oh, yes, terrible, like in Russia.

TOMI: I'll bet it's those gypsies, breaking camp.

SHEILA: What? Oh, no, the travellers are the other side of Clairmont Hill.

ZHENIA: Do you want me to clear it up?

SHEILA: Oh, no, dear. This is definitely the groundskeeper's job […] someone called Learmouth, who obviously doesn't work at the weekend. I'll have to get hold of him somehow. He should have been on my list of helpers.

ZHENIA: This is my friend Tomassina. Everybody just says Tomi. This is Mrs Budgeon, the fete chief.

SHEILA: Chairperson, dear, and I've told you before, Sheila, please. *(To TOMASSINA)* How do you do? Er, *do svidania*. Have I got that right?

ZHENIA: *(Laughing)* Absolutely, only you said goodbye.

TOMI: And I'm English anyway. We live next door from each other.

SHEILA: And your son or daughter comes here. Yes, I've seen you. You're down to be working a […] what kind of stall was it?

TOMI: Same age, but she goes to your bog standard primary school, my daughter.

ZHENIA: *(Quickly)* I thought perhaps Tomi might help *me*.

SHEILA: Well, of course, if you feel you need it. I hope the others will come soon. I suppose we might make a start with the tables, hm? As long as there's no one else here to do it.

She begins to unfold and set up the tables. ZHENIA is quick to assist. TOMI merely comments.

TOMI: Is this going to be like your average school fete, sponge the teacher and that? That was always my favourite.

ZHENIA: What's sponge the teacher?

TOMI: Teacher sticks her head through a hole in the cardboard, then the kids take turns trying to hit her with a wet […]

SHEILA: I shouldn't think Mrs Lockneed would agree to that for a moment, and I wouldn't want to know any child that tried! I hope that's not what you plan to do. I think we must find this man Learmouth. *(She goes off momentarily)*

TOMI: Here, that's not Mrs Lockneed, is it?

ZHENIA: Didn't you hear her just now? – Sheila Budgeon.

TOMI: I think I'd best scarper.

ZHENIA: You said you'd help me.

TOMI: She looks ready to deep-fry me in brine.

ZHENIA: She likes everything *organized*, that's all. But it's all right. You're here helping me.

TOMI: It's more than that. My face doesn't fit. Zoe's school's the wrong side of the level crossing. Do not cross signs wherever you look.

ZHENIA: But it's a party.

TOMI: It's a local village fete. Did anybody tell you about them? Ordeal by water, fire and free-range cream cake, and I'm not having any part of it. You can reach me tonight when all the dust has settled. I'll be at home with a bottle of *Chablis*. No, I won't either. You haven't forgotten you're sitting for me tonight.

ZHENIA: I haven't forgotten; I never agreed.

TOMI: You did, when I asked you on Thursday. Don't pretend now you didn't.

ZHENIA: Mark says I can't anymore. Sorry.

TOMI: The fuck's it to do with him?

ZHENIA: You're joking, of course.

TOMI: Oh, I see. It's all right for *me* to do favours for *you*, because I don't have a boss man to say I mustn't.

ZHENIA: I've done loads of favours for you. I'm always sitting for you, whenever you ask. But this time I can't.

TOMI: Because Mark said so.

ZHENIA: Because it's all night. You want Zoe to sleep at our house, so you can spend the night with your boyfriend.

TOMI: You didn't have to tell him, did you? Coulda said I was going to hospital. That's what English girls say.

ZHENIA: Then ask English girls to watch Zoe for you. I can't do it, for once. And stop pretending it's all on your side, will you? Today was for the last time I babysat Zoe. And now you say you're going. That's not doing what you said you'd do.

TOMI: If I stay, will you think about tonight?

ZHENIA: I'll ask Mark to speak with you.

TOMI: You're a bitch behind the simpering smile, aren't you. You couldn't care less what happens to me. Admit it.

ZHENIA: Please, Tomi. Mark's angry at me as it is. Now my mother's with us as well. I don't know for how long.

TOMI: Don't tell me. I understand.

ZHENIA: Believe me, you don't. His mother wants to take Tanya to live with her.

TOMI: Because of Zoe and me, I suppose.

ZHENIA: No! Because of me – because I'm Russian!

SHEILA returns with a table.

SHEILA: I found them hidden away, you know where? Someone or other's garden shed. I've never even met this man Learmouth, whose shed it no doubt was. I certainly hope he wasn't planning to steal them. No, I mustn't think ill of people just because the ones at the shelter can't always be trusted. *(To TOMI)* I help to run the Wellington Centre, you know.

TOMI: Yes, I've seen it.

ZHENIA: You want us to help bring the tables. *(To TOMI)* Let's go, Tomassina.

SHEILA: Perhaps you and your mate can wait here in case Cyril turns up. I think I'd first better see to the catering. I'm sure Hannah will have turned up by now. Oh, Eugenie. Mrs Lockneed tells me you're working to become a full-time teaching assistant.

ZHENIA: It's hard work. There are lot of essay to write, and my English, you know […]

SHEILA: I think your English is splendid, and what's more, your care for the children is exemplary. I mean, look at today. You're the first one on site, ready to do anything. You'll probably be the last one to leave tonight, too.

TOMI: All right, that's it. I'm off.

ZHENIA: No, wait a minute. Excuse me, Mrs – Tomi, don't go.

SHEILA: Remember to watch out for Learmouth. *(She goes off again)*

ZHENIA: Yes, all right. Tomi, please. What's the matter?

TOMI: I already told you.

ZHENIA: But I don't understand.

TOMI: No, you wouldn't, would you. You're exemplary, not a slag like me. That's what she was saying just now.

ZHENIA: You're imagining it.

TOMI: Oh, yeah?

ZHENIA: She doesn't even know you.

TOMI: She knows me, all right, knows my kid and all. What do you think all that bullshit—

ZHENIA: —please.

TOMI: All right, eyewash, was for. She remembered seeing Zoe and me down at that shelter of hers. She probably reckons we nicked something. She'd never bother to ask if maybe we were victims of domestic violence. We were the scum of the earth, far as she was concerned, and she didn't want nothing to do with us. And now she's said it again by singing your praises for my benefit. I'm exactly the sort that they can well do without. All right, she's told me. I'll see you as and when, as they say. Go, you Christians!

ZHENIA: Zoe can stay at our house tonight.

TOMI: What about Mark?

ZHENIA: You leave me to tell Mark. I'll tell him Tanya wants Zoe to stay with her. Mark can bring them both as soon as it starts.

TOMI: It's not her fault nobody wants her, poor little mite.

ZHENIA: I've got to see about the food. *(Starting off)* Can you stay till the very end, though, as long as we're needed?

TOMI: I'll do you better than that. I'll teach you all about gunge tanks and bash-the-rat.

They pass out of view as COURTNEY and HANNAH come on.

HANNAH: Three dozen cheese and asparagus vol-au-vents. Carrot and celery cup. Those celebrity chefs got a world's lot to answer for. Five different dailies of fruit and veg. This is a party. Kids want flapjacks and turkey twizzlers. And the stuff that comes out of their mouths! Shouldn't be let within broadcasting distance of children. *(To COURTNEY)* Did you manage to find casings for all of them? Courtney, love?

COURTNEY: My William, they say, is a mathematic marvel. He sleeps with algorithms under his pillow. Leastways I think that's what they're called.

HANNAH: Will you straighten up and pay attention? We have almost a hundred expected here soon after midday. And expected means they want to be fed. Mrs Lockneed specifically told me not to count on them eating the exhibits, whatever they are. I said, Does that mean a sit-down meal for some of them? And she said, Well, buffet style. Of course, she's really talking about fully catered, only she wouldn't know that. And it's not our place to enlighten her. This is a school fete, so the school's kitchen's expected to cope. Francine was up till 3.00 helping me.

COURTNEY: William doesn't go to bed either.

HANNAH: Is that any part of this discussion? I'm telling you Francine, my daughter, spent the whole night cooking for this lot.

COURTNEY: Haven't I got the right to be proud of my son?

HANNAH: Not this morning, you haven't, definitely. I'm more than a little fractious about the whole thing, and the best you can do, short of lending a hand, is to measure your words in tiny doses, the smaller the better would be simply ideal.

COURTNEY: I know what you're telling me, don't worry.

HANNAH: Fine […] thank you.

COURTNEY: That Knock-kneed woman has been giving my Cyril no end of grief.

HANNAH: What are you talking about?

COURTNEY: That's what I call her, you see – Mrs Knock-kneed. And he's been onto the council because of the rockslide in back of his house. It's downright lethal, rocks through the roof to his sitting room.

HANNAH: Do we have to talk about this now?

COURTNEY: Well, you were just saying how Knock-kneed exploited your daughter, and I said she was doing the same thing to Cyril. Ringing him at home and then ringing me because she didn't find him at home, of course, he was with me. Only William and Cyril don't get on.

HANNAH: Get on, yes, that's exactly what we must do. Now if you take those vol-au-vents out of number three oven […]

COURTNEY: I know it without you telling me […]

HANNAH: Good. *(Sees SHEILA)* 'Morning, Mrs Budgeon.

COURTNEY: 'Morning.

SHEILA: I knew I could count on you bright-and-early.

HANNAH: Oh, yes, you know, up with the lark.

COURTNEY: She had Cyril patrolling the grounds half the night, which is not his job. They're not even his grounds. He could get hisself arrested and charged for her sake, and who's to say she wouldn't just claim she didn't know him. Mud like that sticks like Lucite.

SHEILA: Who's that you're talking about?

COURTNEY: Shouldn't think you'd know him.

SHEILA: It's not, by any chance, Cyril Learmouth?

COURTNEY: That's right, but what's it to you?

SHEILA: I've been frantically trying to get hold of him.

COURTNEY: He deserves his lie-in after what he's been through.

SHEILA: But he's meant to be *here*!

COURTNEY: All right. *(Gets out her mobile)*

SHEILA: If you could just tell me where he is […]

COURTNEY: He's sleeping over at my house. *(To HANNAH)* Some people want to know everything about a person … William? Is Cyril making a noise? What do you mean, Who wants to know? Stop playing Bugger My Neighbour, okay? Go and look […] Well, why didn't you tell me that before? I swear I'm going to have you sectioned before you see me again. All right, we'll just see who grasses up who first. *(To SHEILA)* William says he's already left. 'Course, that could just mean William's too lazy to fetch him.

SHEILA: But where would he be if he's not?

COURTNEY: Who you talking about, William or – ?

SHEILA: I just need to locate the groundskeeper, all right? There's a mess in that corner that's got to be cleared.

COURTNEY: And you're saying it's Cyril's job.

SHEILA: If he's the substitute groundskeeper!

HANNAH: He'll be in his lodge at the school if he's anywhere on site. Courtney becomes a bit agitated in a rush.

SHEILA: She thinks she's the only one. I agreed to be Chair before they told me it was being held in a field *alongside* the school. And then people don't do what they've agreed to ... or they don't turn up. I've been from pillar to post trying to *find* everyone.

HANNAH: Why're you telling us, love? We've been using a makeshift kitchen since Thursday. I've no idea at all if it's been cleared by Health and Safety. If it's not, who they going to pin it on, me?

SHEILA: Oh, please, don't upset yourself. It's not going to happen to anybody, I *hope.*

HANNAH: You may be Chair, but whose orders d'you think I've been carrying out? Mrs Knock-kneed has to know everything, doesn't she, including what we're expected to wear. One minute it's kitchen gear, next it's—

SHEILA: What did you call her, Knock-kneed?

HANNAH: Oh, I been listening to Courtney too long. You know I don't mean any disrespect, only whose orders am I meant to be following, yours or your […] hers?

SHEILA: Well, I don't think there's a need for *any* of us to be at each other's throats.

COURTNEY, meanwhile, has crossed to greet CYRIL LEARMOUTH, a man with a marked deformity. Some of their dialogue may overlap.

COURTNEY: You didn't cross words with William this morning, did you?

CYRIL: Never seen him.

COURTNEY: Because he's convinced you don't like him.

CYRIL: That's what he thinks about the whole world. I've got to get on.

COURTNEY: But if he thinks you're going to move in with us […]

CYRIL: Then you put him up to the idea, my love.

COURTNEY: But where else can you go? Your house is an absolute tip.

CYRIL: Billy wants his walking papers from you, Courtney darling. I have little to do with it.

COURTNEY: But if we tell them you have to move in, then they'll just have to help William out. You *must* see that, Cyril. It's a roller ball bonus all around if you move.

SHEILA: *(Overhearing)* Cyril? Are you Cyril Learmouth, the groundsman?

CYRIL: I'm the porter of Boniface School, what's your problem?

SHEILA: *(Pointing)* That […] that hideous eyesore is my immediate problem. But then there are the tables […]

CYRIL: I'll make a start on tables […]

SHEILA: *A start? I've been* […]

CYRIL: As to the mess over yonder, it's been sorted.

SHEILA: What do you mean? It's just sitting there.

CYRIL: From the gyppo camp, madam. I've just taken steps that'll settle their corn beef and cabbage.

SHEILA: I don't know what you mean. Are they going to remove it?

COURTNEY: *(Giggling)* You mean you've done something nasty. Did you throw a smoke bomb?

SHEILA: Are you out of your mind? We're a Church school. The Bishop might have us closed down. All I ask is for that mess to be got rid of.

CYRIL: That's just what I was about to do.

SHEILA: Yes, but when? They'll start arriving in less than two hours. And here you are, bad as the vandals.

COURTNEY: You haven't heard he's done anything yet.

SHEILA: Please don't. It's a police matter.

COURTNEY: It's really down to the politicians, but you won't see them getting involved till they need our vote. And what are you giving him orders for? Are you his boss?

SHEILA: I'm in charge of the fete this year; I only asked for his help. I'll get onto the police myself, if you'd rather. We're meant to be getting our own Support Officer for the afternoon.

CYRIL: I've already contacted a private security firm [...] Mrs Charlotte asked me. That's what I meant a moment ago.

COURTNEY: *(To SHEILA)* There now, don't you feel foolish?

CYRIL: Steady yourself, Courtney, love. Everybody's just out for having a good time.

SHEILA: That's all I'm trying to ensure. And that's rapidly getting *impossible.* Can you please, from now on, inform me first of what you intend doing. I understand you're only a *replacement* for the afternoon. Nevertheless—

COURTNEY: Well, I'm sorry. But it drives me wild the way people always take your good nature for granted.

SHEILA: If I'm guilty, then let me apologize. Now can we get on?

COURTNEY: If you really want to help, you can see about getting us a permanent home.

HANNAH: You don't half take the prizes for cheek, Courtney Crumb.

COURTNEY: She runs the shelter for homeless, does she not?

SHEILA: That's right, but is *this* the time?

COURTNEY: The homeless don't pick their time to be homeless, do they? You ought to be used to it.

SHEILA: Are *you* homeless?

COURTNEY: My William soon will be. They're all of them joined at the hip. She could ring up the council as easy as pie. Rachel Darling, a poor handicapped fellow called William Crumb urgently needs to be re-housed. Can you see to it for us? Thanks, awfully. That's how it's done.

CYRIL: Courtney, love—

COURTNEY: Oh, I'm not for a moment suggesting she should, just saying she could if she wanted.

CYRIL: *(To SHEILA)* She gets a bit carried away.

SHEILA: I'm accustomed to dealing with worse, if that's possible. *(To COURTNEY)* One phone call, is that what you want?

COURTNEY: I told you.

SHEILA: *(Looking at CYRIL)* But you said it's your son that's disabled …

COURTNEY: That's right, he's got mental problems. It's all right, he's not on anyone's register. He's afraid to go out of the house.

CYRIL: Oh, yes, her son is a good boy.

COURTNEY: More deserving than many, I'll say that much.

SHEILA: I'll do it, but would you mind if we deal with matters more at hand? *(To CYRIL)* You say the security men are on their way?

CYRIL: I'll make a start on clearing the mess.

CHARLOTTE LOCKNEED comes on.

SHEILA: Thank goodness you got here!

CHARLOTTE: There's no need for panic, is there?

CYRIL: Your friend's worried about that mess over there.

SHEILA: That's not the only thing – there's the weather.

CYRIL: And the tables, you said.

SHEILA: *I've* been doing – Yes, and the tables.

CHARLOTTE: We back on to a travellers' camp, don't we?

SHEILA: Why do you all insist it's travellers? I wasn't aware they were here.

COURTNEY: They're like vermin, that's why.

HANNAH: Can I ask something about the food, please? We have the *vol au vents*, the pasties, the sweet 'n'sour risotto …

CHARLOTTE: The health and safety people!

HANNAH: Excuse me?

CHARLOTTE: They rang up yesterday afternoon. They need to make an inspection.

HANNAH: Well, they can't. Did you tell them the fete is today, not next week?

CHARLOTTE: They say they only want to check the way to the toilet. I never knew this, but it seems it's illegal to use the same passageway to the kitchen that you use for the toilets.

HANNAH: That's right, if this was a restaurant. Did you tell them we're holding a church school fete? Would you like me to do it, ma'am?

CHARLOTTE: I think we'll both have to see them in person.

HANNAH: But we'll be through by a quarter to seven. They're not going to get here before then.

CHARLOTTE: All right, Hannah. You do as you see fit. I'm just passing it on.

SHEILA: What time does the guest of honour appear?

CHARLOTTE: Guest of honour, you mean Grace David?

SHEILA: No one else? I thought you said you had a celebrity booked. Jedward or Cheryl Cole, someone like that.

HANNAH: Or Hugh Fearnley Whittingstall, he could tell me what's wrong with the stew.

CHARLOTTE: But Grace David is the school's patron, and she looks forward so much to it every year. That's acceptable, isn't it?

SHEILA: Oh, yes, that's just *fine*.

CHARLOTTE: Did I tell you this year's theme is Spring Awakening?

SHEILA: Did you bother informing anyone else?

CHARLOTTE: That's not adopting a helpful attitude.

SHEILA: I'm just tired of being in the dark!

CHARLOTTE: There's nothing anyone's kept from you, my dear. This is a Church school fete, not a pop concert. It's perfectly natural to pay tribute to the minister's wife, especially as I understand she's just lost a beloved relation.

SHEILA: I'm not saying she shouldn't be doing it. But did she bother to tell anyone?

CHARLOTTE: I don't suppose she placed a notice about it in the *Church Times*. What's your point, dear?

SHEILA: No point at all! I think I'll just rally the troops. (*She starts off*)

HANNAH: Do you want to look over the provisions, Mrs Lockneed? We made risotto for about 50, cheese and asparagus vol-au-vents, pasties, I'm planning a huge sherry trifle …

CHARLOTTE: But didn't we go through this yesterday?

HANNAH: Just to see there's enough.

CHARLOTTE: And what do we do if there isn't? It's far too late. We'll simply ease them toward the exhibits. That's what they're for. People can't ask too much of school catering when we're already providing the venue.

HANNAH: That's what I said all along.

CHARLOTTE: What's that, dear? I wanted her out of earshot, because I'm sure those gypsies are responsible.

CYRIL: It's what I was saying meself, ma'am.

CHARLOTTE: Ah, yes, but you can't say it in certain quarters, or they'll have you before a Race Relations tribunal. I've tried. Lord knows I was onto the council the minute we discovered the break-in last February. And they fobbed me off. Same with the local constabulary. They'd provide us, they said, with our own Special Constable, and it was only after a week and a half that they told me that meant a volunteer. He wouldn't even be full time. I said, What on earth's the point of that? and I was told, flatly, It's extremely low risk. Nothing of value was taken, it seems, so there was no need for anything else. In fact if I asked for more, I might well be liable to a charge of wasting police time. And then the man instigated a knife search among our pupils. The threat is out there, I said. So then he promptly withdrew. If so, madam, that's where I should be. And that reply, you must be given to understand, goes on yours and my council tax. This is precisely what we pay for.

COURTNEY: And that's precisely why Cyril went private, isn't it, love? He remembers the argy you went through.

CYRIL: If I could spare you, I would do, that's what I said.

CHARLOTTE: Quite right, Neville.

COURTNEY: Cyril.

CHARLOTTE: Of course.

CYRIL: So you don't mind that I took it on myself.

COURTNEY: I said all along how she wouldn't.

CYRIL: They said they'd be here before the fun starts.

CHARLOTTE: Who's this we're talking about?

CYRIL: Northcliffe Security, ma'am. Director's descended from Lord Northcliffe, just to show you their pedigree.

CHARLOTTE: And they're going to do what, Cyril?

CYRIL: Ensure everything is the up-and-up.

CHARLOTTE: Wait a minute, what are you talking about? You engaged a private security firm […] to come here […] this afternoon? But what possessed you […] who gave you the authority?

CYRIL: But I thought […] with the gyppo contingent.

CHARLOTTE: But they're not coming in. They wouldn't dream of it for a moment. All we've got coming are parents […] and […] and local dignitaries. And you want them greeted by bouncers? Are you quite sane? Guest of honour's the minister's wife.

CYRIL: And each one could pass for her son-in-law, I promise you. They all dress like Jehovahs.

CHARLOTTE: Gangsters dress like Jehovahs, Mr Learmouth.

CYRIL: But they look smart as carrots, don't they.

CHARLOTTE: And cost a small fortune.

CYRIL: It's worth it. Besides, this was the first of this year's charitable donations. Lad in year six asked his father to help. An ex-CID man.

CHARLOTTE: What, the man is a parent, you mean.

CYRIL: And a loyal parishioner.

CHARLOTTE: Not that anything's likely to happen.

CYRIL: Can't be too careful these days. *(Points)* Look at that.

CHARLOTTE: All right, I see what you mean. *(Calling)* Can I help you in any way? We're
               about to open our annual school fete.

She is addressing CHLOE and ISLA, who come on from the direction of the pile of rubbish.
CHLOE in particular looks suspect, wearing body art. CHARLOTTE suspects them of
being travellers.

Mr Learmouth, this seems to require a man's presence.

CYRIL: You're on the point of trespassing, dear.

ISLA: But isn't this the St Boniface school fete?

CYRIL: That's exactly what it is. Now why don't you go on back to your camp?

ISLA: We've come to help.

CHLOE: We're part of Zack Drucker's party.

ISLA: Chloe is. My son went here in 1992.

CYRIL: *(To CHARLOTTE)* Do you have a Zack Drucker?

CHARLOTTE: You mean to say you're parents? I'm so sorry.

CHLOE: Didn't you issue an alarm call for volunteers?

CHARLOTTE: Indeed we did, but the way you're […]

CHLOE: It's a fete, right? So I'm going to teach them all face-painting. *(Holds up
               kit)* All right?

CHARLOTTE: Just face-painting? No tattoos?

CHLOE: You want to check me for needles? Not even the stick-ons.

COURTNEY: What about piercing?

CHARLOTTE: Oh, Lord, no, no piercing, for pity's sake. You'll be opening us up to public enquiries.

CHLOE: I wouldn't dream of it. They have it done, though. I get asked all the time. Never guess where one eight-year-old wanted it. I said no, though, don't worry.

CHARLOTTE: She wasn't one of ours […] was she?

CHLOE: Wouldn't know. My Zack didn't know her anyway, but he's in another year group.

ISLA: My son Alan was lost in Helmand Province.

CHARLOTTE: Really?

ISLA: He was a Master Sergeant with the Prince of Wales Regiment.

CHARLOTTE: And he was a pupil of ours!

ISLA: In 1992, yes.

CHARLOTTE: Before my time, of course, but I'm shocked he isn't remembered in our files.

ISLA: I've brought along two of his decorations to show people.

CHARLOTTE: My dear Mrs […] We couldn't possibly accept such a donation.

ISLA: I'm not *donating* them.

CHARLOTTE: I should think not, indeed. Oh, yes, I see what you […] You mean you'd like to exhibit them, in memory of […] what was your son's name?

ISLA: Alan […] Alan Curnew.

CHARLOTTE: It does ring a bell. He must be in the school log.

ISLA: We lost him eight months ago.

CHARLOTTE: Oh […] oh, yes, there was a memorial service. You and I've met before […] at the service.

ISLA: I appeared on the television at the time.

CHARLOTTE: No, but I'm sure at the service we […] saw each other anyway. And nobody mentioned that he was an Old Boy.

ISLA: He attended for only one year.

CYRIL: I'd better see to all that mess.

COURTNEY: I'd better help you.

CHARLOTTE: *You* remember him, don't you, Mr Learmouth?

CYRIL: They pay me *not* to pay close attention, if you follow me, ever since the Ian Huntley case.

CHARLOTTE: Well, yes, I know, but […]

CYRIL: *He* was on television. Reporters were all day asking, And what do *you* think happened? Pays not to notice a thing.

COURTNEY: *(Following him off)* So what do you think, they're accusing you of something? Cyril, wait […]

HANNAH: And she's meant to be helping *me. (To CHARLOTTE)* Suppose I'd better wait for the H and S brigade […] and try to conjure up another passageway.

CHARLOTTE: No, I think you're probably right, they're not coming.

HANNAH: That's just how they're likely to turn up. Excuse me. *(She starts off)*

CHLOE: Is it all right if I set up anywhere here?

CHARLOTTE: Your son, too, is an Old Boy?

CHLOE: Uh-uh, he's a *new* boy. Zack Drucker, year five.

ISLA: His father fought in Iraq.

CHARLOTTE: But he's all right.

CHLOE: He's still living, if that's what you mean.

CHARLOTTE: Then he'll be here this afternoon.

ISLA: He's […]

CHLOE: No, he can't make it today. *(Looks at ISLA)*

CHARLOTTE: Well, no, if he's off in Iraq. Sergeant Drucker. Such an awful business.

CHLOE: Why? What have you heard?

CHARLOTTE: Aren't they bringing them home now? Such a terrible waste. He's not injured.

CHLOE: He's up on a charge of serious misconduct.

CHARLOTTE: Ye-es.

CHLOE: I mean it – he and his mates are facing not only a court martial—

CHARLOTTE: I'm sure it's a terrible mistake. Zack's father would never disgrace any of us.

CHLOE: Would you rather I left?

CHARLOTTE: Left? Certainly not. Don't let them go wild with paint, though.

ISLA: I brought two dozen apple turnovers.

CHARLOTTE: *(Drifting off)* Lovely.

ISLA: Why did you tell her about Steve?

CHLOE: To stop you from doing it. You were going to, admit it.

ISLA: I'd have said he was away in Iraq.

CHLOE: And she'd have seen straight through that.

ISLA: She'd never have said anything. Now you've just made it harder for Zack.

CHLOE: Suppose you let me and Zack cover that, okay?

ISLA: I don't believe it anyway.

CHLOE: Oh, *I* do. There's not a doubt in my mind that's what Steve and his pals got up to on the q.t.

ISLA: Stop it, Chloe.

CHLOE: I'm not talking about your lad. The PWR, everyone knows they're the elite. Steve is just a dog soldier, so why shouldn't he behave like a dog.

ISLA: I don't care to hear any more.

CHLOE: Fine. And call me every name you can think of, but at least you'll never have the job of explaining your husband to his son, like I have.

CHARLOTTE and SHEILA come back on, as do TOMI and ZHENIA.

TOMI: Dumplings? No one's going to want them when they have Cornish pasties.

ZHENIA: But there's no meat.

TOMI: Exactly, and they're not sweet. They'll end up as food for the dog.

ZHENIA: But what else have I to sell?

TOMI: Gawd. They didn't impose a target on you, did they? Give you some mortgage-like figure you'd have to make up yourself if you couldn't meet it?

ZHENIA: No! They never said anything like that.

TOMI: Are you sure? Your English isn't that sharp.

ZHENIA: You're just trying to make scandal.

Overlapping:

CHARLOTTE: If you're absolutely bursting with it, I'd be a fool to stop you.

SHEILA: I think that's putting it a bit steep – bursting. You make it sound like […]

CHARLOTTE: We all know what it *sounds* like. That reminds me. Disabled conveniences.

SHEILA: What?

CHARLOTTE: Do they have them this side of the wall? Where's […]? Mr Learmouth? Cyril? Hannah? Sheila Budgeon wants to address you all, and *I* need to find out about loos.

COURTNEY: Cyril's on the phone to those security men.

HANNAH: I still don't see what we can do. The second exit is to a back garden. The best I can do is bring all the food out.

CHARLOTTE: I'm not really talking about that.

SHEILA: Can't they just use the ones at school? I didn't know we had any disabled.

CHARLOTTE: Somebody's chair-ridden granny? Of course, we have. This should all have been plotted out weeks ago, not the very morning of the event. Well? Are you going to address them?

SHEILA: Is this *my* fault? It's *your* school, after all. Do you want me to mention it?

CHARLOTTE: And how are you going to do that? Portaloos, anyone?

SHEILA: That's a thought.

CHARLOTTE: One that's best kept to oneself. *(Speaking up)* Can we have your attention, please?

SHEILA: *(Consulting a clipboard)* This is more of a final checklist. I'm delighted to see you've all turned up on time.

CHARLOTTE: But they haven't *all*. Isn't that very much the point? Some don't even belong to us.

SHEILA: But we're very glad to see you just the same. Er, I hope the good weather holds up anyway. I'm sure it will. I don't seem to see any men about yet.

CHARLOTTE: […] because there aren't any, obviously.

HANNAH: Fred Epsy took his family to the country.

CHARLOTTE: What do you mean, *we're* the country. We're competing, I hear, with the annual food-and-livestock fair. A lads' weekend in Newquay sounds far more likely to me.

SHEILA: Be that as it may – I'm simply … delighted to find so many willing hands and hearts …

CHARLOTTE: Oh, Sheila, please, this isn't the Duke of Edinburgh awards. The weather's going to be kind to us, we *hope*, and a handful of willing helpers have turned up on time.

SHEILA: And we hope there are more in the offing.

CHARLOTTE: Yes, quite.

SHEILA: And the theme of this year's fete is Spring Awakening. *(To CHARLOTTE)* Have I got that right?

CHARLOTTE: Perfectly, dear.

COURTNEY: *(To HANNAH)* Here, what's with those two?

HANNAH: Can you not guess? Oh, never mind. You're right that there's something. They're sisters, but they don't want anyone to know it.

COURTNEY: No! I don't believe – Here, Hannah says the two of you are sisters.

SHEILA: *(Laughing)* That's perfectly ridiculous!

CHARLOTTE: I never heard anything so […] so absurd.

HANNAH: What did I tell you?

CHARLOTTE: Does anyone have anything *useful* to contribute?

SHEILA: We're supposed to have a convenor for the pledges – is that right? Someone looking after the money we raise. And I've already disqualified myself.

CHARLOTTE: A mercy for us all. *(To SHEILA) Merci.*

SHEILA: It's not right one person should do it all.

CHARLOTTE: I count one, two […] eight people here and several more on their merry way.

ZHENIA: *(To CHARLOTTE)* I thought you asked Mark to be chief.

SHEILA: And again you didn't bother to inform *me*.

CHARLOTTE: Does it really matter for the moment?

SHEILA: This is exactly how two or three people end up doing the lot.

ZHENIA: But I did tell you. My husband Mark. Don't you remember?

SHEILA: Heads a building society or something.

ZHENIA: He's the town surveyor.

SHEILA: Is that it? Just as long as he's doing it. He *is* doing it.

ZHEILA: He's reliable. You said *I'm* reliable, didn't you.

SHEILA: Oh, of course, dear, I didn't mean […]

CHARLOTTE: I'm sure he's the man of the hour. Knows exactly who's going where and why, long before the rest of us have even woken up to the fact. And he'll be here *presently.* Isn't that right?

ZHENIA: He's coming along with our children.

SHEILA: Well, I don't suppose he's needed till later. Now Grace David. You say she's opening the festivities.

CHARLOTTE: At half-twelve, that's right.

SHEILA: And no one in tow.

CHARLOTTE: *You* want the Duchess of Cornwall or Rowan Williams's wife.

SHEILA: He hasn't got one […] and someone like that takes months of preparation. I just wanted to know.

COURTNEY: Is this a family confab or can anyone kibitz?

This may be a cue for the dialogue to overlap.

SHEILA: Someone just needs to tell me the final plan. Right, so Grace David opens proceedings, with a prayer? 'Ode to Joy', something like that?

ISLA: Has anyone thought about a military band, some sort of tattoo, perhaps?

SHEILA: That, too, should have been sorted out *weeks* ago. Now […] Grace David.

CHARLOTTE: She'll say what she has to say, for God's sake. She's the vicar's wife. Does she need to say anything?

SHEILA: Not at all […] The local college drama group have promised a performance of sorts.

CHARLOTTE: Wonderful, as long as it's not *Pyramis and Thisbe*.

SHEILA: I think they said a version of *Pirates of the Caribbean*. There are loads of bit parts for the boys.

TOMI: I've got the greatest stall game for us – Asteroid Blaster. You get a piece of fruit or, better yet, an egg and the kids try to knock it down with water pistols.

ZHENIA: Everything will get all wet […] my dumplings.

TOMI: You're committed to them, are you?

ZHENIA: My mother's making them now. She's going to bring two dozen more in an hour or two.

TOMI: What game do you want them to play, Fairy Princess?

ISLA: What do you think you're doing?

CHLOE: *(Painting her face)* Giving your face a little lift.

ISLA: Nothing too garish now.

CHLOE: What about a Union Jack?

ISLA: No, certainly not! I mean [...] it's a bit too young for me, don't you think?

CHLOE: This *is* a school fete, yeah?

ISLA: Yes, I know, but [...]

CHLOE: It's the one time in the year you *don't* want to look your age.

ISLA: Couldn't we make it a nice fleur-de-lys?

CHLOE: All right, where, across your bum crack? *(Grins)* I'll put it right there on your forehead.

COURTNEY: Can you do me next? Something from Harry Potter, maybe.

CHLOE: The Truly Wicked Witch? Sure.

COURTNEY: I was thinking maybe [...] Hermione Granger.

CHLOE: You're too old for the part.

HANNAH: Let's get this straight. You're definitely finished helping me?

COURTNEY: No, I'll do whatever you want, only [...]

HANNAH: Only you're busy right now.

COURTNEY: You said you'd speak up for me, remember? *(Nudges her)*

HANNAH: What, right now?

COURTNEY: She's standing there.

HANNAH: Mrs Lockneed, Courtney wants to be a teaching assistant.

COURTNEY: Not that!

HANNAH: Well, what do you want?

COURTNEY: That's the same as saying William wants the Nobel Prize for Physics.

HANNAH: I dunno what you want me to do.

CHARLOTTE: I think I understand.

COURTNEY: You're supposed to speak up for me!

CHARLOTTE: Why don't you have a word with Zhenia Norris? She's midway through the training.

COURTNEY: You mean she's got the inside track?

CHARLOTTE: How long have you been working here?

Sudden shot from an air rifle.

CHARLOTTE: Now what on earth!

COURTNEY: Oh, God, he's been shot. I know it – those gyppos have murdered him.

HANNAH: You don't even know it was gunfire.

SHEILA: And why must it always be gypsies?

COURTNEY: But you saw him. He went over there.

CHARLOTTE: Who's this she's talking about?

HANNAH: Cyril Learmouth.

CHARLOTTE: That's right. He said he was going to clear up the mess.

COURTNEY: And they went and shot him for it.

CHARLOTTE: Well, is there any way we can find out?

CYRIL: *(Approaching, struggling for breath)* Bleeding maniacs […] begging your pardon, ma'am.

CHARLOTTE: Are you all right?

SHEILA: What was it, exactly?

CYRIL: What? Those thieving […]

SHEILA: Oh, please don't say gypsies […] was it?

CYRIL: *You* want to try and confront them?

SHEILA: Not especially. Perhaps they just didn't know […] I mean perhaps they were frightened. That can make people very aggressive.

CHLOE: How many were there?

HANNAH: And they fired on you.

COURTNEY: They can't claim trespass. You can have them for attempted murder.

CHARLOTTE: Just a minute.

COURTNEY: And then you can get compensation.

CHARLOTTE: I said wait a minute. *(Thinks)* Compensation from whom? What are you talking about?

COURTNEY: Injured at work. The school has a duty to make good.

CHARLOTTE: Are you out of your mind, woman? You've just asked us all for a job. Now you want to take us to court?

COURTNEY: What's right is right.

CHARLOTTE: Exactly. Nobody's injured. We don't even know yet what happened.

COURTNEY: You wouldn't say that if it was *your* husband. *And* Cyril's disabled besides.

CYRIL: I'm still in one piece.

CHARLOTTE: That's what I was saying.

COURTNEY: Next you'll be saying it's his own fault.

CHARLOTTE: Oh, shut up, please.

CHLOE: What kind of weapon was it?

CYRIL: An air rifle.

CHLOE: Are you sure? They don't even fire real bullets.

COURTNEY: Here […] why don't *you* keep your mouth shut!

SHEILA: This is hardly helping.

CHARLOTTE: Are you hurt at all? I want to get that clear.

CYRIL: I told you. He missed me completely.

CHARLOTTE: Well, *that's* a relief.

CYRIL: I'll think twice about going back there, though.

CHARLOTTE: Quite. *(A beat)* And you don't want to claim against the school.

CYRIL: Claim what? I don't follow you.

CHARLOTTE: It doesn't matter. *(COURTNEY humphs)* As long as you're all right. That's the main thing.

SHEILA: Somebody should put up a warning sign for this afternoon.

CHARLOTTE: Oh, yes, of course. We must.

COURTNEY: Suppose you want Cyril to do it.

KACEY comes on to noticeable effect. She walks slower than average, with the aid of crutches or sticks. She is dressed as a gypsy fortune-teller.

KACEY: Who's been shooting at who?

COURTNEY: From the look on your face, Kacey, love, they might have been shooting at *you*. You all right, are you?

CYRIL: *(Helping her)* Why don't you come over here, love. *(He positions her at a chair behind a table/stall near CHLOE and ISLA)*

CHARLOTTE: The fete hasn't actually started yet, my dear.

KACEY: Didn't you ask for volunteers?

SHEILA: You mean you want to run a stall – splendid!

CHARLOTTE: And you're somewhat *disabled*, aren't you!

KACEY: What's that to do with anything?

CHARLOTTE: You'll be wanting, at some point, *to use the loo*.

SHEILA: We're just wondering about people using the nearest facilities.

KACEY: Me, you mean? I'll go next door, at the school.

SHEILA: Thank you. That's just what *I* said.

KACEY: Of course, the kids from Hephaistos may need something more.

SHEILA: Kids from [...] *where* did you say?

KACEY: Hephaistos, local school for disabled kids.

SHEILA: I wasn't aware that they'd been invited.

CHARLOTTE: No, *you* thought everybody'd be entered for the egg-and-spoon!

SHEILA: Just how severely disabled *are* they?

CHARLOTTE: Enough to need porta-potties, obviously.

KACEY: So you're saying they can't come.

SHEILA: Of course not, but […]

TOMI: Wait a minute. What's the problem – taking them back and forth? Eugenie and me can do it between us. *(To CHLOE and ISLA)* Maybe you two can lend a hand.

SHEILA: It's not only that. I've heard that Down's children are apt to turn violent when excited.

TOMI: Where'd you hear *that*? And aren't you the one that thinks gyppos are hard-done-by?

CHARLOTTE: What sort of a stall are you running, my dear? You look terribly exotic.

KACEY: Fortune-teller. I read tarot cards.

CHLOE: Great stuff – we'll be the Exotica Corner.

CHARLOTTE: What sort of things are you going to say?

KACEY: I practise the Marseilles version – about love, fortune, fate. Each card represents a temporal guide, like, for instance, Behemoth would take you on your journey toward great wealth […]

CHARLOTTE: […] or maybe success in their level three exams?

KACEY: This isn't a joke.

CHARLOTTE: No, but it *is* a school fete, and these are children. *(To CHLOE and ISLA)* You see my point.

CHLOE: All right, but they idolize Harry Potter.

KACEY: Jessica believes in it absolutely. Our lives are controlled by The Tarot.

CHARLOTTE: But couldn't you confine your predictions to going on a school trip, perhaps?

COURTNEY: Your Jessica's year group is going on one next Wednesday.

KACEY: No, they're not.

COURTNEY: Year three? I'm sure I got that right. They're off to Tintagel. I know because Eugenie and me are going as helpers. That's right, isn't it, Genie?

ZHENIA: I thought it was later than that.

SHEILA: And it may be another year group altogether.

ZHENIA: No, it's Tanya's year group. I should know.

HANNAH: And that makes it Jessica's, too.

SHEILA: You mean it might be.

HANNAH: I'm sure it is, just don't ask me why.

KACEY: But I *am* asking; I've every right to know.

SHEILA: How can Hannah know for sure?

HANNAH: I'm providing the food, that's how. And I was told, in particular, that one little girl wasn't going. If it's only a rumour, then Mrs Lockneed here can deny it.

CHARLOTTE: I know what this is about. *(To KACEY)* Can we discuss this on Monday, the two of us?

KACEY: I want an answer now.

SHEILA: But the fete's going to start!

CHARLOTTE: Is it possible your daughter's autistic?

KACEY: My daughter's fine [...] she's effing marvellous, in fact. What are you doing discriminating against her?

SHEILA: No one's—

KACEY: She's just admitted it. She knows all about it. I *don't*. What's the story?

TOMI: She's a whiter shade of pale, that's all. They don't want to see her.

ZHENIA: What do *you* know about it?

TOMI: My Zoe's the same. She's not popular, so she's a speckled egg. Things happen, and *she* gets blamed. She's a bully, her mother's a tart.

ZHENIA: But her daughter Jessica – I'm sorry to say this – Tanya's frightened of her. Please don't ask me to explain. But [...] she didn't want to go if Jessica went, too.

HANNAH: And she's not the only one, my dear. More girls than I can count told me they felt exactly the same.

COURTNEY: I can't seem to place who you mean.

SHEILA: She's not disabled, is she? Maybe she couldn't cope.

HANNAH: *(To COURTNEY)* You know her by sight: crop top and leggings, a Jessica Simpson hairstyle.

COURTNEY: Not *her. (HANNAH nods)* She ... threatened to do something to me—

HANNAH: What? If you didn't do what?

COURTNEY: No, no, for nothing. She was just *mean. (To KACEY)* She couldn't be *your* daughter.

HANNAH: She has to be *somebody's.*

The following two-handed exchanges overlap:

ISLA: Does your son know the girl they're talking about?

CHLOE: He never talks about his friends. Never brings anybody in the house.

ISLA: If she's bad, then they shouldn't allow her at school.

CHLOE: She's a charity case, though, she must be. How could her mother afford the fees?

ISLA: That's true. Alan's grandparents paid his. Edward lost his job as a building contractor, and I had to work at Tesco's to pay the bills.

CHLOE: Maybe they'll ask us to remove Zack once the trial is over.

ISLA: You can't think about any of that.

CHLOE: Why? It's not going to disappear.

Overlapping:

ZHENIA: She's not at all like your Zoe. If she was, do you think I'd say anything against her – honestly, me? Come on.

TOMI: I'm just saying I know how she feels, that's all.

ZHENIA: I *didn't* speak out against her. Even when Tanya told me what she does.

TOMI: What does she do? You can't point the finger and then keep stum.

ZHENIA: Can't you imagine?

TOMI: Oh, that's very good. You leave it to *me*. All right, no. I'm a complete novice. Tell me. Does she threaten to lace her, with a razor?

ZHENIA: No!

TOMI: Or punch her arm black and blue. That's what she'd get in the State sector.

ZHENIA: All right [...] she spat at her.

TOMI: Is that all? How, a hairy gob of a spit?

ZHENIA: I don't want to talk about it.

TOMI: Did she really wallop her one? *(Hits her)* Like this, was it? *(Hits her)*

ZHENIA: Stop it! *(Beat)* She called her a Russian. *(TOMI says, Aw!)* A dirty Russian.

Overlapping:

CHLOE: Your son can never grow up hating his father – you can always get to sleep at night knowing that.

ISLA: I'm sure he doesn't hate [...]

CHLOE: No, wait [...] I want to tell you.

ISLA: Please don't.

CHLOE: It wasn't a form of Post-Traumatic what's-its they had. Please don't, for God's sake, think *that*. My husband's guilty, all right? He had [...] they molested three Arab boys between them, no excuses. My father-the-bum-bandit, that's what my son's got to live with the rest of his life. He's a paedophile, not a hero, a fucking *nancy* paedophile.

ISLA: We're meant to be having a party!

CHLOE: Oh, yeah, I just wanted to make that clear.

CHARLOTTE: *(To KACEY)* I'd like this discussion in *private*, if you don't mind. On Monday even. I owe it to you.

KACEY: I'm not having a discussion ...

CHARLOTTE: But your daughter is clearly *disturbed*.

KACEY: Too right she's disturbed, she's *discriminated*.

CHARLOTTE: But we had to take steps.

KACEY: *I'm* the nutter, all right? The disabled one. You leave Jessica where she is […] she's fine.

CHARLOTTE: She is not fine […] she attacked a child many times smaller than she is … punched and kicked her. And then pulled down a little boy's pants, just to have a look, terrifying the poor little chap. She's the school *bully*, if you must know. We rarely get them. We've *never* had any like her, I must say.

KACEY: So why is it only coming out now? Whyn't you tell me before?

CHARLOTTE: Because of your condition, quite frankly. We wanted to give this the widest berth, er, every chance. But we couldn't hold out any longer.

KACEY: You know what's going to happen, don't you, if she's not on that coach […]

CHARLOTTE: I know what will happen if she *is* […]

KACEY: I also practise the Abysmal Tarot, you know what that is?

CHARLOTTE: We're back to Potterland, are we?

KACEY: *(Looking at CYRIL)* This man Learmouth is the driver, isn't he? He's also The Fool. There's more than a good chance an accident will happen. And he's also lame. He's perverted with evil lame thoughts.

CYRIL: Here, you stop that now.

KACEY: No, perhaps not an accident but *something* unexpected, something sinister. *(To CYRIL)* Please don't put them at risk.

CYRIL: I'm not the driver. Now why don't you get off home. Stop annoying these good people.

KACEY: Well, what are you doing here? It's very unlucky. *(Of COURTNEY)* And she, definitely, shouldn't be here. *(To COURTNEY)* You've appeared as an omen, haven't you, you and your partner – look. *(Turns over a card)* Male and female demons – the devil in human form.

COURTNEY: Think *you* must be some kind of malign force … that daughter of yours is a *changeling*.

KACEY: Why? Because you took photos of her […] on your iPod?

SHEILA: Oh, please. Can't we all just be *friends*. Look, Grace David is coming, now quiet.

KACEY: And your partner in sin […] the bus driver. Getting children to reach in his pocket for money […] whenever he feels the urge.

COURTNEY yelps.

COURTNEY: *(Becoming hysterical)* It's not true … nothing about it is even partly […] she's lying, I tell you […] I never …

HANNAH: I know. No one believes her. It's all right. *(To CYRIL)* I'll give her something to calm her down. *(To COURTNEY)* You'll be all right, my love. Nobody pays her any attention. *(They go off)*

CYRIL: *(To KACEY)* You like to hurt people the way you've been hurt, but it ent right.

CHARLOTTE: Don't provoke her. *(To KACEY)* Just don't speak to the children like that. They don't deserve it. If you want, I'll think about cancelling the trip. *(To CYRIL)* Can you make yourself available for the next half hour?

CYRIL: I'm here for whatever you want, the whole day.

GRACE DAVID comes into view.

SHEILA: *(Covering)* Hallo, Grace, dear. We're all so happy to see you. Today's forecast is very promising – Well, we hope it's reliable. All things willing, you'll be able start the proceedings in—

GRACE DAVID wears a simple dress.

GRACE: I'm not going to be able to attend.

SHEILA: Oh, dear, no, really? Oh, but you've had a recent bereavement, is that right?

CHARLOTTE: You did know you were starting us off.

GRACE: Oh, yes, that's why I'm here.

SHEILA: I don't see how we could impose, in a way.

GRACE: But it's not a bereavement.

SHEILA: Oh, well, that's a relief.

GRACE: No, in some ways it's worse.

SHEILA: Really? Well, I'm sure you don't want to *talk* about it.

GRACE: Oh, no, I *want* to talk about it […] need to […] very much.

SHEILA: But not now perhaps.

CHARLOTTE: I'm sure we can get someone else, in the circumstances.

TOMI: *(Overlapping)* What's all this fucking about?

GRACE: As long as you don't feel I've left you in the lurch. But Duncan, you see, has been arrested.

CHLOE: Not another one!

ISLA: Shh!

TOMI: *(Overlapping)* Up the Christians! Let's hear it for the cannibals!

ZHENIA: *(Overlapping)* Shut up.

KACEY: *(Overlapping)* Behemoth has started to speak!

CYRIL: *(Overlapping, still ministering to COURTNEY)* Maybe it all ought to be called off.

COURTNEY: *(After the others)* I never did anything like what she said.

CHARLOTTE: Quiet […] all of you!

SHEILA: Shouldn't we really speak about this in private?

CHARLOTTE: That'll only set the tongues wagging.

GRACE: What do you mean?

SHEILA: *Well* […]) Oh. Oh, yes, I see. No, it's nothing like that. I don't even know if you could call it arrest. He's been summoned by the Bishop.

SHEILA: That's not so bad, is it? Not bad at all necessarily!

GRACE: He's going to be asked to resign. You remember he got on the television last week. They asked him about economic conditions. It was very unfair really. It's well known they're not allowed to ask questions like that. The answers should carry no weight. And he said, in certain circumstances, it was better to steal.

ISLA: Oh, I remember this. As soon as he said it, I thought […]

GRACE: It's […] it's ridiculous, really, he was deliberately led on. He was trapped.

SHEILA: But don't they have advisers?

GRACE: Who're you talking about? Someone from the Bishopric heard about the broadcast, obviously, and he rang us up! Was Duncan serious in what he said? Well, are you serious about your belief in God? Of course, Duncan repeated he meant what he said. He would have retracted it otherwise. Well, did he quite realize what he'd said? It was getting quite anxious at this point. The official didn't really identify himself. Was he speaking ex-officio? We didn't know.

CHARLOTTE: But the police were never involved. In any case.

GRACE: The police?

CHARLOTTE: He hasn't been arrested and charged with anything!

GRACE: He's losing his parish, isn't that enough? Asked to go on extended sabbatical after which he'll leave the ministry. Where do you suppose he'll go from there, botanical gardening? Perhaps he'll become local history archivist […] required to log our demise. I'm so distraught.

SHEILA: Would you like to sit down over here? Can I get you some water?

GRACE: What sort of thing do you want me to say?

SHEILA: You mean you're staying?

GRACE: I came here to tell you I couldn't, didn't I. I think I'll be able to manage if I don't have to manage a lot.

SHEILA: Well, no, a simple spring-time Biblical verse.

GRACE: What, the voice of the turtledove […] something like that?

SHEILA: Exactly.

GRACE: 'And the voice of the turtledove […] throughout the land […] Arise, my darling, my beautiful one […] come along!'

SHEILA: That's not in the Bible, is it?

GRACE: Song of Solomon: 2:12.

SHEILA: (To CHARLOTTE) Of course, this is all *your* fault – Spring Awakening! I think we'd do better with something from the Jabberwocky, do you know Lewis Carroll?

TOMI is doing something with drugs.

ZHENIA: What do you think you're doing?

TOMI: Freebasing cocaine.

ZHENIA: Are you crazy?

TOMI: What, this dozy lot? They'll think it's fish paste sandwiches.

ZHENIA: Mrs Lockneed is right over there! And my mother! Hallo, Mum!

TOMI: (Sarcastic) Yeah, right. Along with *my* mother and Dame Vera Bloody Lynn.

Her mother GALYA and IRINA (a Russian friend a bit older than ZHENIA) come on bearing trays of dumplings. TOMI may utter a surprised expletive and more as the women rush to put the trays down without much notice of her business.

GALYA: It's a blessing Irinichka came by when she did. I'd have had to make two trips by foot. With my back, that would have finished me.

IRINA: Chance for me, too. I was coming by to find out if you knew the minister Duncan David. Galusik said he'll be here at the fete.

TOMI: Wait just a min-ute, willya? They ent gonna disappear.

IRINA: But you don't know. These are heavy and they are hot.

ZHENIA: I don't know if he will, but his wife is right over there.

IRINA: Where […]? That woman? I want to tell you before telling her. You remember I told you we were having our kitchen remodelled. Well, he came, and we've had nothing but chaos for ten days. Pipes burst and water all over the floor.

ZHENIA: My God.

IRINA: That isn't the end of it. Workman said he won't move until we pay him at least one third. But we can't pay him *anything*. Our clients, including the Church, don't pay *us*.

GALYA: But it's just like my flat back in Russia. Liuba's mother, our neighbour put in new flooring in their flat above us. But it's tile flooring, not wood, and it's possible to hear *everything* – you know, pee-pee, as it goes in the toilet, and *(Simulates sound of orgasmic excitement)* when they're making love. I told her about it before I left, and she became very angry. But she rang me up frantic this morning from my flat. She's been staying there while I've been here. And what do you think? She can't sleep either. She can't concentrate. She's going mad.

TOMI: Your mother's here, right? You don't need me.

ZHENIA: Are we going to go all through that again?

TOMI: No, we're not. Zoe's home alone.

ZHENIA: But Mark's bringing both girls. I told you.

MARK: *(Coming on)* Mark's brought them. They're over at school.

TOMI rushes off.

Overlapping:

GRACE: *(To IRINA)* But I don't understand what you're saying.

SHEILA: And *I* don't understand. Did you come here to help with the fete?

IRINA: I came here because of her husband, the vicar.

SHEILA: But she's had a terrible shock with her husband.

IRINA: And I know why. But we've had a terrible shock, too. We've no money and massive bills to pay. And it's *his* fault.

GRACE: He didn't rob you, did he?

IRINA: A form of robbery, yes, exactly.

SHEILA: And he boasted about it on television!

IRINA: What are you talking about, television?

SHEILA: Perhaps you'd better explain what *you* mean.

IRINA: *(To GRACE)* Your husband hired my husband and me to audit the Church's accounts.

GRACE: You're accountants?

IRINA: And he's defaulted. We have bills to pay. Of course, we know precisely how he's defaulted […] But my husband suffers from angina, and this only makes him worse.

GRACE: But the reverend isn't your only client, surely.

IRINA: He's a big one. I was told two or three others would be here today. I don't see them.

GRACE: And you won't see him either. He's been arrested.

SHEILA: […] called away on Church business.

IRINA: If he's gone into hiding or fled the country, he'll be discovered.

GRACE: He's already in police custody.

SHEILA: *(To IRINA)* You should be ashamed.

IRINA: Because I'm a foreigner? He did it himself. I don't understand life in this country – massive overdrafts, credit-card debt. Back in Russia, we have to pay. My mother, 80 years old and alone in Siberia, needed workmen to repair her leaked roof. Two-hundred rubles, they told her, and they wanted it first. Oh, don't worry, she told them. My daughter's in England. *She'll* pay. If you have a daughter in England, our price is R800.

SHEILA: I really don't see—

IRINA: Wait! I'm trying to tell you. The old lady's now dead.

GRACE: I'm so sorry. Pneumonia?

IRINA: Murder. *(A beat)* It's true. Later that night, while she was sleeping, thieves broke in and beat her to death. She had no money, but how could they know? For them, England meant money, and they killed her for what she *didn't* have. Perhaps you can see why I'm perhaps oversensitive on the subject of theft. Especially when it is advertised.

GRACE: My poor darling.

Overlapping: FERN TOMSETT comes on in floral attire. CHLOE immediately reacts. SHEILA crosses to greet her.

SHEILA: Mrs Tomsett, er, how good of you to come.

FERN: I've brought a floral display. I hope that's all right.

SHEILA: How delightful […] apt! *(Looks for it)*

FERN: An arrangement of Biblical verses in daffs and tulips – they're at the back of my husband's estate car.

SHEILA: Then he'll be needing a hand. Cyril? Mr Learmouth?

FERN: What I need to know first is how close to the tent we can drive.

SHEILA: As near as you're standing, give or take!

CHLOE: They didn't come from a funeral home, did they?

FERN: I beg your pardon?

CHLOE: You don't remember me, do you?

FERN: Yes […] if you just give me a minute.

CYRIL: Do you want me to back her in?

FERN: If you can! *(Gives him the keys)* The forest green Vauxhall Meriva!

CYRIL: I see 'er! *(Goes off)*

SHEILA: You ladies will lend a hand, won't you.

CHLOE: Of course we will! That's more than her husband would do for us.

FERN: I'm sure I don't know what you mean.

SHEILA: Please, ladies, let's not have bitter words.

CHLOE: Bitter, me? I'm only too happy to help! I'm even ready to believe it wasn't her fault.

FERN: Did my husband offend you in some way?

CHLOE: His bank turned me down for a loan.

SHEILA: No business or politics […] please!

FERN: It's out of my husband's hands anyway, but I'm *sorry*.

CHLOE: Well, my money is out of his bank.

FERN: I daresay I'd feel the same.

CHLOE: That's decent of you. And you're off on your annual holiday, I expect. Canary Islands, no doubt.

FERN: What sort of business was it?

ISLA: No, don't humour her – she doesn't deserve it. *(To CHLOE)* Three others turned you down as well.

CHLOE: That doesn't stop her from going abroad, from living there probably. On her husband's fat bonus. And what are you doing defending her? You couldn't afford the school fees. If the bank held the mortgage on your house, you'd be out. You'd be asking *her (SHEILA)* to house you.

FERN: No, she's right. I am genuinely sorry. You probably wanted to start a dressmaker's shop.

CHLOE: B and B [...] on the edge of Dartmoor.

FERN: I'd have backed you. The worst of it is, I happen to know of a pub/hotel that was financed by us. Same location [...] and run by a man. You're divorced [...] or a widow, perhaps?

ISLA: *(Jumping in)* Her husband's away in Iraq.

CHLOE: He *was* in Iraq. Now he's on his way to prison! *(FERN: Ah!)*

ISLA: He wasn't when you applied for the loan! They discriminate against single women!

CHLOE: And she still takes her holidays on time.

Overlapping:

GALYA: Oh, lapichka Mark, don't blame Zhenia, it's not her fault. It's mine, my fault completely. I'm a complete idiot, completely. My son bleeds me dry, he worries the brains right out of my head

ZHENIA: Oh, please, Mama, can't you give it a rest for Mark's sake?

MARK: Tell your mother I'm not going to speak Russian to her anymore. She's plain stupid. Can you tell her that?

ZHENIA: She's just admitted it.

MARK: She's been here for seven months now [...] and not three sentences of English.

ZHENIA: She's going back.

MARK: She asked me to run this online advert – complete with our name and address. They'd be queuing at our door. We might as well shine a red light in the window. Do you wonder my mother's concerned? Is that how you want your Tanya brought up – Any man who lives near to my daughter.

ZHENIA: She didn't mean it.

TOMI: *(Returning)* The gate's locked, and nobody answers the bell.

MARK: Oh, they're in there, all right. Along with a teaching assistant, Hazel Lantz. But I wouldn't be all that anxious to disturb them. There's also a Community Support Officer, who'd be sure to search you for drugs. One look at your nose would be all he'd need. *(To ZHENIA)* My mother also told you to be careful in choosing your friends.

TOMI: I want to get out of here!

MARK: I don't blame you. But wait a bit, eh? This isn't going to take long.

KACEY: I knew this would happen, you see? I knew it. I turned over Justice, numbers eight-11. First she *(Pointing to IRINA)* came, and then him. *(Points to MARK)* Who's next, do you think? And what will they do? What recompense will they seek?

MARK: Will you all just keep it quiet a minute?

KACEY: He's stern, isn't he. Looks like with him there's no half measures [...] no turning back!

MARK: Look, you asked if I'd keep track of the money for you. I thought you might want to know where you stand. If you're not really bothered, then fine, I'll get on with my own life.

SHEILA: Of course, we're bothered, we're very grateful. Wasn't I just saying before you came?

MARK: Do you want to hear this?

SHEILA: Are we starting now? We're not going to wait for the children?

MARK: They're over the way at the school. They're fine. I thought you might all profit from hearing this. You, too, Mrs Lockneed. I promise the children are safe, and you need to hear this – it concerns the future of St Boniface.

CHARLOTTE: But this isn't a Governors' meeting [...]

MARK: It's a fete, I know. And the Governors voted on holding the fete, in spite of the crisis.

KACEY: The omens [...] the impending doom.

MARK: Shut up, will you. I'm being perfectly serious. The situation calls for it.

Sound of screeching brakes, followed by

CYRIL: Bloody hell!

COURTNEY: I knew it – he's injured a child!

CYRIL: *(Off)* Never touched 'er [...] she's all right.

CHARLOTTE: *She?* I've got to see what's happened. *(She starts off)*

MARK: *(Calling after her)* The school's nearly bankrupt, you know!

SHEILA: A child may be seriously injured.

MARK: Our children are seriously injured every day. But perhaps you don't care. Perhaps you're not even aware of the cost they extort from you annually. The fees rival the public schools once you average things out.

SHEILA: Oh, please do shut up.

CALEB: *(Falling on)* Bloody hellfire and farts aflame!

KACEY: Another demented cripple!

CALEB is lame and carries a unicycle. He's drama-student age.

SHEILA: Are you injured?

CALEB: No, as far as I work out […] not even a broken stride.

SHEILA: But you're limping.

CALEB: That, I'm pained to inform you, is the result of a crooked pair of forceps applied to my foetal self. I've come to entertain the kiddos.

SHEILA: You're part of the drama troupe […] are you. And you're performing a pantomime.

CALEB: I thought I was here on my own – unicycle.

SHEILA: Is this all of you? We expected a troupe. Not that we're not grateful …

CALEB: I do have a socialist magic act I can go into at will.

SHEILA: Oh, dear, no, no politics, please […] I'm sure your […]

CALEB: […] my unicycle […]

SHEILA: […] will be just fine.

MARK: *(Overlapping)* I've asked Charlie Penge to address us! He's also Councillor Penge to some of us […] and Chairman Penge to those supporters of our local Spartans. Does that arouse anyone's interest?

SHEILA: We've asked Grace David to open proceedings.

MARK: Ah, but I'm talking about beforehand. Charlie?

CHARLES comes on from the direction of the street, supported by CHARLOTTE LOCKNEED.

He's been seriously injured!

CHARLOTTE: I don't know how to apologize.

CHARLES: Please don't bother […] no need, no need at all.

CHARLOTTE: That […] absolute clot of a caretaker.

COURTNEY: I don't suppose he did it on purpose.

CHARLOTTE: What difference does that make?

CHARLES: Look, he never touched me, all right? I saw him backing up and […] missed my footing.

MARK: We're all mightily relieved to hear that. We'll give you a moment or two to rest. Give him some room to the front.

CHARLES: I'm all right. What's going on here?

CHARLOTTE: Our annual fete […] You mean you didn't know.

CHARLES: Of course, I was planning to come along later. You're not holding it *now*, are you? *(To MARK)* You just said you wanted a meeting […] a Trustees' emergency meeting, is what I understood.

MARK: These are better than Trustees. They'll hang on your every word.

CHARLES: In that case, no, I'm here as a private citizen […] a Friend of the Fete, nothing more.

CHARLOTTE: Exactly, we've inconvenienced you quite enough.

MARK: But as long as you're here […]

CHARLOTTE: No, I refuse to be part of some underhanded plot.

CHARLES: Plot? You make it sound like an ambush of some sort.

MARK: Exactly. Nothing of the kind. Mr Penge came here of his own volition. Missed his footing, it's true. But we're all apt to do that in life. He's here to help us usher in the spring.

CHARLOTTE: We're not quite ready to open yet, are we?

SHEILA: And I thought Grace David was doing the honours.

GRACE: Oh, don't worry about me.

CHARLES: What sort of things do you have planned? Egg-and-spoon races?

SHEILA: Yes, I think so and, er, exhibits of various dishes.

CHARLES: And a raffle? Oh, you must have a raffle. You must let me contribute.

SHEILA: We're not going to put you to work.

CHARLES: Whyever not? I'm on the Governors' board. I should have been here from the start.

SHEILA: I don't think we wanted to bother you.

CHARLES: Well, it's true I'm not easy to get. But you managed to get me here. So now what can I do? I'm Chairman of the Spartans, did you realize that? We could offer a season ticket as the grand prize […] offer a whole range of tickets, why not?

MARK: Are they going to be in existence next season?

CHARLES: 'Course they are, what are you on about?

MARK: I thought they were going belly up.

CHARLES: Here, you're not some fucking reporter, are you?

MARK: Me? I'm a town surveyor.

CHARLES: (Grunts) Well, we never been healthier, I'm telling you.

MARK: Never had it so good?

CHARLES: *(Beat)* I know who you are. You're an Eagles rep, aren't you. This is a bloody wind-up. Ha! I don't know when our fixture is, but I'll tell you right now. We're going to scalp you for this. No half measures. You know what I mean?

MARK: Absolutely. And we'll be waiting for you.

Overlapping:

CALEB notices KACEY.

CALEB: Hallo, sweetheart. I didn't know your kiddos went here. Didn't know you had kiddos. I've seen you round, of course. Always wanted to make myself known.

KACEY: *(While looking at cards)* You're speaking disabled speak.

CALEB: Yeah, all right. I'm not a piss artist anyway. I'm not coming onto you. You might be hooked up with a Ewan McGregor type.

KACEY: You've come here today to create crippled havoc.

CALEB: Me? No, I just came to entertain the kids. I've recently mastered the unicycle and somebody said they'd go ape – like it very much. Maybe I could cycle all day for a couple of tenners. I'm a poor student.

KACEY: I know – I've seen you begging in the underpass: Handi and Homeless.

CALEB: Did I take the piss out of you? Maybe *you're* homeless. Maybe you stay in a shelter for cripps. I came over to say hallo.

KACEY: You're probably on a B-Tech drama course where all they want you to do is play a silent and *gay* Richard III. Tell me I'm wrong and I'll give myself to you like Lady Ann.

CALEB: You don't have to do that. *(Looking)* Ah, I see. You read the Tarot. Did you hear me say I do socialist magic tricks. You probably think that's pretty naff.

KACEY: And I tell you you're going to do something extraordinary here today – something that will make your fellow students think they should have offered you portions of Hamlet.

CALEB: I don't mean to cut off your flow. But don't get me arrested, you know? We've been sharing a squat for the last seven weeks, and we think the council are onto us. If I'm not careful, they're going to haul me in, and then *I'll* have to go into sheltered housing. Those places aren't Spanish resorts.

KACEY: I'm sorry. I dropped my card. *(He bends down for it)* What card is it?

CALEB: The beggar!

KACEY: Nat-ur-ally! (Seizes him and kisses him violently)

CALEB: Do you want to go for a drink […] somewhere?

KACEY: Please, darling, you have work to do.

CALEB: I don't understand what you mean.

KACEY: You must make yourself known to *everybody! (HANNAH and COURTNEY come on)* These two, for example.

CALEB: Hallo, there […] My name's Caleb. I'm—

KACEY: He's the Health and Safety Officer you've been told to expect.

HANNAH: I told you before nobody believes you. *She* won't believe you from now on.

CALEB: *(Not quite in control of what he's saying)* As long as she learns to believe me.

HANNAH: *(After taking him in)* You're a friend of hers, aren't you.

KACEY: He made himself known to me only today. *(To CALEB)* You say the porta-pots are […] where did you say?

CALEB: I didn't—

CHARLOTTE: *(Overhearing)* I think I should be in on this discussion.

CALEB: We need to feel, if there are going to be disabled kiddies on site, that they have ready access to the lavatories.

KACEY: You can use me as a test case. I'm as disabled as you're going to get. And I'm not going to mess with any Franco-freak porta-pot, thank you very unkindly. I'm going to go where it's private, so's every other disabled bod I know. We'll fight our way over the road. But I suppose you now want to talk about kitchen access?

CALEB: I do? *(Whispers)* It's not me saying any of this.

KACEY: You don't know your own strength.

HANNAH: *(Suddenly attuned)* Look, I'm sorry. But we didn't have any advanced warning about access. I thought that was only for restaurants anyway.

CALEB: I'm not here to talk about access. *(Whispers)* Too right I'm not. You're making me say things I don't feel.

KACEY: I'm making you the life of the party.

CALEB: We've been led to suspect there are vermin in the foodstuffs.

COURTNEY lets out a scream.

CALEB throws a toy rat at them both and KACEY laughs.

Overlapping:

CHARLES: *(To IRINA)* I seem to detect a slight trace of accent. Are you […]?

IRINA: […] Russian.

CHARLES: Russian!

SHEILA: She came to us altogether unannounced with a quite extraordinary tale about—

CHARLES: And your name is […] Don't tell me too quickly.

IRINA: Birt-whistle.

CHARLES: I don't understand.

IRINA: My husband and I are accountants. Are you the same Charles Penge who also heads the local council?

CHARLES: Yes, but don't flash it round. Chairman of Biddlescombe FC is enough of a handful for one afternoon.

IRINA: I am not surprised you want to keep quiet about your affairs.

CHARLES: I don't like spreading myself too thick. It's not English, you know. We're not Russian oligarchs […] playing Monopoly for real.

IRINA: No, oligarchs are far too good at their jobs […] even when caught. They always have *something* salted away.

SHEILA: Will you please stop annoying the guests? I don't want to turn anyone away, only you must act appropriately. As Mr Penge says, this is England.

CHARLES: No, no, no offence taken. This young woman's just got the wrong end of the stick. There's no need for anyone to fall out over anything, is there?

IRINA: We're not falling out. I'm trying to track down a bill.

CHARLES: A bill *I* owe?

SHEILA: Oh, *please.*

CHARLES: No, no. You're perfectly right, of course. *(To IRINA)* This isn't the time or place […]

IRINA: This is *exactly* the time.

CHARLES: I see. *(As though to an unbalanced woman)* We could always take steps to have you forcibly removed. You're upsetting everyone's enjoyment. But okay, I understand. You want this settled immediately.

IRINA: I want you to admit to something you've done.

CHARLES: You're not in league with this gentleman, are you? *(Motions to MARK)* Working together to trap me in some way? In any case, here is the name of my solicitor, all right? You ring him on Monday, everything will be sorted out.

IRINA: Including your bogus pension scheme?

CHARLES: Everything. I'm terribly sorry.

IRINA: You will be, don't worry. What about those shares in Icelandic banks that ratepayers invest in without knowing?

CHARLES: Ah, now you're making accusations. Serious claims before witnesses, eh? Very dangerous ground. And you a foreigner. You think you'll be able to back them up? I'm here among friends I've known all m' life. Our families go back generations. And who are you? Some unpronounceable heathen? An interloper? Maybe you're even a vagrant. Your home has been repossessed.

IRINA: Because people like you can't settle their accounts. We're all part of the new homeless melting pot!

Overlapping:

GALYA: Lapichka, you must make it up with Zhenia. She loves you more than the tongue in her head can tell you in Russian.

MARK: Everything's fine between us.

GALYA: You mustn't blame her for my shortcomings. I'll leave here as soon as you want me to.

MARK: This is not why I came here today. Do what you want. Try to marry the first man you see, only don't expect me to support you.

GALYA: Don't blame Zhenichka, I beg you.

MARK: Let go of my arm.

ZHENIA: *(Coming forward)* Quiet, Mama. Mark has things he has to do.

GALYA: Leave me alone!

She breaks away, and MARK makes a beeline for IRINA. PENGE, in the meantime, has gone to speak with GRACE DAVID.

MARK: *(To IRINA)* I saw you confront him. What did he say?

IRINA: He didn't admit anything. Who are you? He pointed you out to me. What's your involvement in this?

MARK: I'm with a team of surveyors.

IRINA: So do they owe *you* money? It's all connected […] every part of it.

MARK: I know. We have a line on the movement of every property in the area […] what's going where and who put the pieces together.

IRINA: And *we* handle their books. They think we don't see anything, but come on. We see it even before they do. We're supposed to report it. *(Seeing SHEILA)* She's connected. Runs a hostel for the dispossessed. She has to know how they got that way.

SHEILA: Look, if you're not actually running a stall […] *(To IRINA)* And I know *you're* not.

MARK: But you put me in charge of the fete revenue.

SHEILA: You volunteered. And you're married to Zhenia, I couldn't have been more delighted. Such a willing pair of hands.

MARK: So I'm here.

SHEILA: But there's nothing for you to do for the moment! We haven't started. There's nothing for you to collect. I certainly didn't engage you to make speeches at people and antagonize the honoured guests. That much we've already got […] from the lager louts next door. They've already fired on one of us.

MARK: You're lumping me in with a lager lout?

SHEILA: No, not exactly.

MARK: Perhaps you'd like to frisk me for Class A weapons.

SHEILA: Oh, don't be such a sensitive idiot.

Overlapping:

KACEY: *(Motioning to FERN)* Try her next.

CALEB: Her? I don't know her.

KACEY: Of course not. But her husband's bank refused to recognize your student grant. Instead of giving you perks as a student [...]

CALEB: That's right. *You* owe me an explanation, sweetheart.

KACEY: She was sunning herself in the south of France.

CALEB: More than anything else, you owe me an apology.

FERN: I'm truly sorry.

CALEB: That's not nearly good enough.

FERN: My husband's not to blame.

CALEB: How do you know he's not? He's the manager, isn't he? So I had the manager called out to deal with me. I had an account at his bank. She's wrong there. I had a perfectly good one, in credit. And I tried to withdraw 50 quid. But this arsehole of a clerk didn't like my looks, resented that I had money and he had to serve me. You don't have an account with us, he said. That's not the account's signature. So the manager – your beloved, I guess – comes out from behind the partition and escorts me personally to the door. You understand how it is, old chap, he says like a favourite uncle. Well, I *don't.*

CHLOE: Me neither.

KACEY: Keep out of this. You wait your turn.

FERN: Yes, of course, I know what you're saying. You imagine I *don't.* That [...] ridiculous protocol is our whole marriage in miniature. That's how he takes me to bed and [...] *defiles* me.

CHLOE: And what, exactly, does that do for us?

FERN: But I'm doing penance here, for *his* crimes.

CHLOE: Yes, and that makes *you* feel fine.

FERN: *(Holding up documents)* What do you think these are, Bible verses, share certificates? You ought to recognize them – look. Applications for small-business loans. Signed and notarized … just fill in the blanks. I'm going to put these in a raffle, but here, take your pick.

CHLOE: *(Looking one over)* I'll bet these are bogus.

ISLA: What's the difference? What have you got to lose?

KACEY: You might need it for other things anyway.

CHLOE: Now I can think about leaving for good.

KACEY: You've still got a score to settle.

CALEB: I don't know her either.

KACEY: You know *him*. Didn't he importune you as well?

CALEB: I don't think so.

KACEY: You may not want to admit it, of course. Who would?

CHLOE: It's not my problem anyway. He's over 21.

CALEB: Well, whoever mentioned consent? Him and his perverted mates attacked me one night outside a disco. I was beaten up […] then I was—

KACEY: Now it's coming out.

CHLOE: How long ago was this?

CALEB: I don't know.

KACEY: Don't be ashamed to admit it.

CALEB: After his other crime anyway. Last time he was on home leave. I tried going to the police about it, but one look and they said it was my fault.

CHLOE: So what do you want me to do about it?

CALEB: Back me up. Maybe bring a charge yourself of domestic abuse. Did he even try it on with your son?

CHLOE: Try what on? Are you crazy?

CALEB: It's all coming out at the trial, you know, questions like that, maybe worse.

CHLOE: What's your game, eh? Just what do you think you're playing at?

KACEY chortles.

CALEB: Me? Nothing. Why? What did you think I said?

CHLOE: *(To ISLA)* Did you copy what's happening here?

ISLA: How could you?

CHLOE: Eh? It's not *me*—

ISLA: And here I've defended you all the way along. Now I'm even ashamed to think I know you.

CHLOE: What, you think I'm best mates with Fred and Rose West? He's an absolute nutcase. *He's* the perv.

Overlapping:

Again the sound of screeching brakes.

An injured WILLIAM CRUMB comes on from the road. CYRIL follows, stun.

CHARLOTTE: How many more have you injured or maimed?

CYRIL: I promise you, nobody. I never touched a one. Billy, you know me. I'm the world's careful driver [...] not a penalty point to my name.

CHARLOTTE: Congratulations – you bagged 12 at once.

CYRIL: Tell her, will you?

CHARLOTTE: No […] *you* can tell the police. They're waiting to interview you.

CYRIL: Yeah, but they want to see Billy, too, don't they? He's a witness […] and a character witness. How about it? You'll stand by me, won't you, Billy Boy?

WILLIAM: What, all crippled queers together? I'd like to see the back of you for good.

CYRIL: You don't mean that. You and me and your mother have always been like a team – a first-rate, honest-to-goodness family. And God knows there's few of those about.

WILLIAM: And what makes you think we're like any of those? My mother's three weeks short of being sectioned. *I* can't leave the house without feeling scared. Hawking and Friedrich want my views on the Atom, and *she* thinks I ought to join a finger-painting class.

COURTNEY: I just said we should have them round to tea […] since you're still a bit wobbly on your pins.

WILLIAM: These men are world class. You think they're Bill and Ben?

COURTNEY: They're consulting you, aren't they? They can move better than you can.

WILLIAM: One of them can't.

COURTNEY: How do you know?

WILLIAM: He's in a wheelchair.

COURTNEY: Is he in need of council assistance?

WILLIAM: You really haven't a dickey-bird of an idea, have you.

COURTNEY: I'm still your mother, and I know you need looking after. I'm sure those others are fine.

WILLIAM: The one in the wheelchair needs constant care. He can't speak except through an electronic voice box. It's a synthesizer

COURTNEY: Don't blind me with science, all right? You don't want them coming here. Maybe you're that much ashamed of me.

WILLIAM: They wouldn't come!

COURTNEY: I got you a council flat!

WILLIAM: So you're kicking me into the street,

COURTNEY: *I'll* take it, all right? As long as you're undisturbed. That's all's in my mind.

CYRIL: Are one of you going to stick up for me?

COURTNEY: Just a minute, love. William and I are sorting something out.

CYRIL: And they're getting ready to sort *me* out [...] with a custodial sentence. Are you happy for them to do that?

WILLIAM: I think your boyfriend is going to jail. Mum?

COURTNEY: Don't be ridiculous. He's coming home with me, either at home in the flat or this lady promised us another flat. I leave it to you to decide.

KACEY: *(To CALEB)* Do you want to say something right about now?

CALEB: What, act as his character witness?

KACEY: I practise Abysmal Tarot – it's a crippled curse.

CALEB: Then I'd rather not have any part of it. These people are crippled enough. You ought to know how that feels.

KACEY: Sod's Law. You mean you want me to *help* them? But look at him, will you? He's right for it.

CALEB: He's never hurt anyone, apart from himself.

KACEY: Oh, shit.

CALEB: What's the matter? It's not going to hurt you this once.

Perhaps some form of special effect.

WILLIAM: I'll find my own way back, Mum.

CHARLOTTE: Mrs Learmouth? Cyril? Police say you're free to go.

CYRIL: Is that right? Well, then, what would you like me to do?

CHARLOTTE: Don't you think you've done enough for one day? You've been fired on by vandals, accused of child abuse, nearly awarded a maximum dozen […]

COURTNEY: And it's not even your regular job.

CHARLOTTE: She's right about that. I should get on home, the pair of you. You can come back this evening to clear up.

COURTNEY: Hang on a minute. William? You see that woman over there with the feather boa? She's the one I saw about your new flat. If you tell her we're related, you won't have to do any more. She'll do the rest. She gave me her promise.

WILLIAM: I'm not going to go there tonight.

COURTNEY: It's all right, love. We're too tired to make love anyway.

WILLIAM: Didn't anyone tell you children hate their parents' intimacies? *I* tell you often enough. Why do you think I want to leave?

COURTNEY: I grew up in an orphanage, remember. That's probably why I forget. What if the bod in the wheelchair phones?

WILLIAM: Tell him, Lift up thy bed and walk.

CYRIL: Let's start wending our way, love, before we need to start coming back.

They start out.

Overlapping this ISLA lets out a scream.

ISLA: My Alan's GC!

CHLOE: What?

ISLA: My son was awarded the George Cross for bravery. I want to know what
                you've done with it.

CHLOE: I ent done nothing with it; I never seen it.

ISLA: That's a lie, for a start. I saw you eyeing my display.

CHLOE: I also heard them telling you you're a fool for putting them out there like
                that. That's just asking for it.

ISLA: So you admit you've taken it. Give it back now and we'll say no more
                about it.

CHLOE: And if I don't, 'cause I haven't got it? *(To FERN)* Do you believe this woman
                for sheer bloody cheek? I'm guilty of incest. Next I'm a thief. After that,
                what? I broke wind at the Cenotaph, maybe peed in the bushes behind
                her son's memorial.

ISLA: I never said any of this. I asked […] merely asked. If you said you haven't
                seen it, that's the end. *(To FERN)* But you can see where I'm coming from,
                can't you? A woman who wears her husband's disgrace so insouciantly,
                then appears to condone it even more.

CHLOE: Oh, yeah, she has to be guilty of every crime going – petty theft, child
                molestation. I can use the five guinea words, too.

FERN: Personally, I never think of wearing anything that wouldn't be better off
                in my husband's safety deposit box.

CHLOE: Personally, I couldn't give a rat's arse.

ISLA: You must have heard me say how valuable it was.

CHLOE: I heard someone tell you how stupid it was to put them out there, *on
                display*. Couldn't you at least get a replica? They retail at something under
                £50.

ISLA:	I wouldn't have thought it was necessary at a church bazaar.

CHLOE:	That's a wet one. Didn't you know that poor-box theft is Ireland's number one crime?

FERN:	Maybe it just fell to the ground.

CHLOE:	How many times have we been back and forth? Believe me, it's in somebody's second-hand gift shop by now.

CALEB:	*(Aside, in a whisper)* Isn't it?

KACEY:	You wouldn't expect me to leave the scene totally unblemished, would you? Who would you like to see fingered for it – the Forces Widow herself? An insurance scam? Look at that tight little Tory kisser, just waiting for someone to tear it apart. Contort it with teardrops, what do you say?

CALEB:	Why not let them just discover it, somewhere? They'd suffer enough.

KACEY:	Oh, but that would signify redemption, and my creed doesn't countenance that. No, there has to be someone at fault.

CALEB:	You weren't thinking of me, were you, because I wigged out with the Terrible Trio?

KACEY:	I'll see how you measure up over the course of the afternoon.

CALEB:	Your daughter isn't coming here, is she?

KACEY:	Absolutely. Who else has her power to make them squirm? Shall I make you her chaperone?

Overlapping:

PENGE with IRINA, GRACE DAVID and SHEILA; MARK with ZHENIA and TOMI. KACEY and CALEB hover between the two groups, CHARLOTTE confers with HANNAH, GALYA and WILLIAM CRUMB find each other.

CHARLES:	I think I have to announce something *(To IRINA)*, is that right?

IRINA:	Pretend you're addressing the Soviet – everyone applauds, nobody listens.
GRACE:	Oh, but I have to speak to them first.
SHEILA:	Think we better had. We called her out in extraordinary circumstances. *(To GRACE DAVID, hoarse whisper)* Remember, though, dear – Jabberwocky.
GRACE:	Dear devoted parishioners – the Right Reverend Duncan, your pastor, cannot be with us today […] because he's been cooking the books.
SHEILA:	Oh, no, she wasn't supposed to say that!
GRACE:	He's made a right reverend mess of the whole lot […] a right bloody shower!
SHEILA:	Is she drunk? No, she couldn't be. Get her off, though, please somebody. She'll ruin everything.
CHARLES:	It's ruined already. We've all had a hand in it.
GRACE:	Your fundraising pledges that you thought went into Mission for Africa and new dedicated pews were actually sunk into Icelandic banks.
CHARLES:	She'll only make it worse. *(To GRACE DAVID)* That's all right, dear. They understand.
GRACE:	No, I've got to confess his many transgressions.
CHARLES:	Careful you don't start confessing to things he never did. *(To the crowd)* It's all right. She's just using religious hyperbole. By transgressions, she means financial, not carnal. Your sons and daughters are perfectly safe from his clutches. I mean, that's just it – he doesn't clutch.
MARK:	He admitted on national television that, in his view, it's all right to steal. What was that, covering his back?
CHARLES:	He was quoted out of context and ex-officio. Good Lord, man, he's not the Pope. It was a two-minute radio interview, all right […]? And he was

talking about you lot. *(Pointing at KACEY and at CALEB)* At you [...] and you [...] and people that live at her *(SHEILA'S)* shelter!

MARK: And he could be next!

CHARLES: I'm not going to argue with you [...] yes, he could. So could we all, every one of us. Like she *(IRINA)* said, it's a melting pot ... to cope with the worldwide financial meltdown.

ZHENIA: *(To MARK)* What did you say to my mother to make her go off half-crazed?

MARK: Please, I'm trying to pin him down.

ZHENIA: I don't give two-and-twenty good fucks! I'm talking like English girls now [...] like she *(TOMI)* taught me.

MARK: That's exactly why I want my daughter out of here.

ZHENIA: She's my daughter, too.

MARK: No, you relinquished that claim when you let her start mixing with daughters like hers *(TOMI'S)*.

TOMI: You just watch it, you bastard.

MARK: I started looking for track marks up her arms.

TOMI: Yeah, right. The kids that go here are angelic, we all know. Her *(KACEY'S)* daughter's nominated Britain's Kindest Kid. They had to hit her with an ASBO last week. I'm not putting up with any more of this shit. I'm getting Zoe out of here now. *(Starts off)*

ZHENIA: *(Follows her off)* I don't think Mark meant it personally [...] Tomi?

CHARLES: *(As though he's been talking throughout)* There's more than you know to the catchphrase, 'Mum goes to Iceland.' High Street chains go there, too. We've been living on Iceland's munificence for more than a decade, and now that's finally bottomed out. We've been ignoring the warnings for years. The rates of return have been just too good to be true. But my friends, fellow townspeople, believe me, please. Some of us have kept our heads during all this. We always knew we were taking big risks. And we bought CDS bonds along with the bank shares as insurance against this disaster. That means, in the main, that you're covered, you haven't lost a thing.

IRINA: So you can make good your standing orders.

CHARLES: I never said I couldn't. Just [...] submit your invoice and we'll honour it in full.

CHARLOTTE: Wait a minute. Somebody [...] you (MARK) said the school's going under. What's the truth of that? Are we all being shifted to Reykjavik?

KACEY: I put a curse on you all [...] I haven't lifted it.

CHARLOTTE: I'm not talking about silly nonsense. Your daughter can go. I'll make her class monitor, if you like. If the coach slips down an embankment or something, don't say it was my fault.

Overlapping:

WILLIAM CRUMB approaches SHEILA. GALYA hovers.

WILLIAM: My mother said you might have a room for me.

SHEILA: What? I'm trying to listen to very important information, and you come at me [...]

WILLIAM: My mother! Courtney Crumb! She works at this school in the kitchen!

SHEILA: I'm not deaf.

WILLIAM: Maybe you're mentally challenged.

SHEILA: I know who you mean. What about her? I think she's already gone home!

WILLIAM: I know that [...] I saw her off! She said you had a room for me. Was she telling stories again? She's always playing *that* game.

SHEILA: Do you have any idea why we're shouting? I can hear perfectly well. Can you hear me?

WILLIAM: Yes, I can […] perfectly.

SHEILA: Fine. She sort of said you were disabled. Are you? I thought she was talking about the other man.

WILLIAM: Cyril Learmouth? Oh, yes, I'm far worse than him.

SHEILA: I find that hard to believe, but we'll let it go for the moment. Are there two of you? *(GALYA)* Do you suppose you could wait till we finish up here?

WILLIAM: As far as I know there's just one of us – me.

SHEILA: *(To GALYA)* But you need a room, too, is that right?

GALYA: Zhenia mother me. *(Pointing)* Zhenia daughter me.

SHEILA: You mean my. What, she's your daughter, Eugenie?

GALYA: *Da..da* […] *pravilna.*

SHEILA: Oh, my goodness, what's going on?

GALYA: Divorce […] they divorce […] me kick out.

SHEILA: Oh, my goodness. But this is terrible. What's going to happen to […]? Then all three of you need a place […] You want a small bedsitting room at the very least.

GALYA: I marry with this […] *(WILLIAM)*

WILLIAM: She's mad. I never saw her before.

GALYA: My son-in-law Mark said I had to get married or he'd divorce Zhenia. That can't happen. So you and me will get married, I'll look after you fine, and we'll have the life that God intended for us. You'll see. Every man ought to have a Russian wife.

WILLIAM: I don't even understand what she's trying to say […] not one syllable.

SHEILA: I think you all ought to sort out your domestics and then come and see me. I'm fairly sure I can help, but I need to know exactly how many you are. Is that fair? Now you'll have to excuse me.

GALYA: *(Grinning, her arm round WILLIAM in Russian)* We'll go home together. I'll keep you warm.

WILLLIAM: We could at least get ourselves introduced before you started the other stuff. My name's William Crumb. I'm a physicist and I'm afraid to leave home. Are you – what are you, Russian? I'm familiar with the work of many famous Russians – Fedorovich, the late Ginzburg, Lev Landau, I'm especially close to Lev Landau.

GALYA: I'll fatten you up, too, with my dumplings and pancakes and sour cream […]

Overlapping:

MARK: I told you, I called this emergency meeting. I convened it. For the best of reasons […]

KACEY: Wait, before you go on.

MARK: I'm not waiting.

KACEY: I want to place in domination […] I mean in nomination […] a replacement fete VIP. We've seen what the ones we got now are. She *(GRACE DAVID)* said it – a right bloody shower! So I propose the following Fete King and Queen and Court Jester – him and her and him […] Come forward, celebrants!

WILLIAM CRUMB, GALYA and CALEB cross to the front.

There are perfunctory cheers.

MARK: All right, but before we get on with anything like a school fete, I think it's imperative to find out if we still have a school.

ZHENIA: *(Coming on)* Excuse me, Mark […]

MARK: I'm determined to get this thing settled.

ZHENIA: Yes, I realize that. But Tomi and I were just over at the school. We had to climb the gates [...] and then break a window. There's nobody there.

MARK: What are you talking about? Of course, there is. Twenty or 30 kids, including Tanya and [...] her daughter. I left them all with a woman named Hazel Lantz. You know her. You trained as a teaching assistant with her.

CHARLOTTE: Exactly, what does she look like?

MARK: What do you mean? She's—

CHARLOTTE: Because there's no Hazel Lantz on my staff.

ZHENIA: And no one named that on my course.

MARK: Well, all right, I got the name wrong. She gave me another one.

ZHENIA: But who is she?

CHARLOTE: And the children [...] What have you done with the children?

Final fade.

Part Two

Essays

Fear into Laughter

James MacDonald

Mikhail Bakhtin develops his theory of Carnival principally in two works, *Problems of Dostoevsky's Poetics* (1963) and *Rabelais and His World* (1965). The latter, famously, extends the theory to book-length proportions as the author traces Carnival back to medieval civilization and applies it exhaustively to Rabelais's magnum opus. But in the book on Dostoevsky he covers the topic in a succinct, fifteen-page essay that gives the reader a concise and easily applicable definition. He begins by calling Carnival 'a syncretic pageantry' whose properties are both 'complex and varied' and whose language 'has worked out an entire carnival sense of the world'. He goes on to describe Carnival as

> ... a pageant without footlights and without a division into performers and spectators. In Carnival everyone is an active participant, everyone communes in the carnival act. Carnival is not contemplated and, strictly speaking, not even performed. Its participants live in it, they live by its laws as long as those laws are in effect; that is, they live a *Carnivalistic life*. Because Carnivalistic life is *life drawn out of its usual rut,* it is to some extent 'life turned upside down,' 'the reverse of the world' (*monde á l'envers*).

> (*Problems*, p. 122)[1]

Carnival Texts' twenty-first-century theatrical appropriation of Bakhtin's theory does not attempt a strict correlation of the various elements. But even a general application brings Bakhtin into a postmodern world that acknowledges the theory's historical origins while advancing it well beyond even the outer limits of Bakhtin's iconoclastic frame of reference.

To begin with Bakhtin's blurring of the distinction between performer and spectator, each of the plays in this informal trilogy seeks to minimize the distance between audience and performer. In *Strangers To Paradise*, audience and spectator meet at the start in the carnival setting that renders identification difficult. The audience is not immediately certain that the people speaking are not boisterous spectators unwilling to settle down. Thereafter, the promenade staging deliberately encourages the audience to remain close to the performers, quite as though they are invading the performance space. In *Brides, Bombs and Boardrooms*, the audience are guided through the action by a compère who effects to speak on their behalf at a Reality-style performance in which they eventually participate. And in *Fete*, again, the audience find themselves at a festival where they are encouraged to see themselves very much as participants. The performers address them as visitors to the bazaar, offering them food, games of chance and fortune-telling. The performance style in all of the plays enhances this proximity through the complete removal of the fourth wall and the performers speaking directly to the audience as another character in the performance.

Even in its present-day form, Carnival is central to all three plays. *Strangers* takes place on Midsummer Day and Eve, beginning at a town-twinning ceremony to commemorate the part Poland played in Britain's Second World War triumph. Significantly, it is also Poland's Feast of St John. Insofar as the action takes place over the course of the day and evening, everything that happens is a part of the festival – from the town-twinning ceremony, to the various attempts of the locals to engage with the East Europeans. In *Brides*, the action culminates in an event in the New Town square where, again, British and foreign residents engage with one another. And in *Fete*, the annual Church school bazaar brings together a cross section of British and foreign participants, each intent on being significantly involved in the proceedings.

A Bakhtinian reversal of the usual order is effected in each of the plays. In *Strangers*, formal decorum is subverted by the Polish mayor's demand of £400,000 compensation for treating his forebears not as allies but as prisoners of war (p. 12), a note of criticism that is repeated in each of the subsequent scenes where the Europeans are belittled, even when they are allowed to remain, only to assert their authority over the British at the end of each scene, to illustrate the transforming effects of the East European diaspora. In *Brides*, the reversal takes the form, initially, of a clandestine mixed marriage between the disabled ne'er-do-well heir to a family fortune and a Russian with possibly criminal family connections. When the son is disinherited, he forms a desperate alliance with a Muslim terrorist for the express purpose of blowing up the town centre financed by his family. In Fete, the anodyne children's bazaar becomes an impromptu emergency council meeting at which shady dealings are exposed. The play ends with the apparent disappearance of the children, intimating that their innocence has been betrayed.

Bakhtin speaks of 'a new mode of interrelationship between individuals' in the course of the Carnival encounter (*Problems*, p. 123). In *Strangers*, this is represented by the partial acceptance by the British of the East European immigrants, an acceptance that includes a partial engagement with different customs and habits. So Polish produce from a local Polish shop is freely available in the street and at the shop's grand opening on St John's Eve. The opening is not merely the beginning of trading. The day's festivities are continued at a party in and round the shop. Drinks and food are served, Polish folk music is played. What began as a British event where the East Europeans are quasi-criminals has become a European-hosted event on their national day, at which they might be seen as the dominant culture, especially when a rowdy British visitor demanding equal rights of work is turfed out. It is also significant that the local police presence is represented throughout by an officer of Polish extraction. The play ends with a private meeting, during the war, between a Polish refugee housed in a prisoner-of-war camp and a young disabled Englishwoman. Hierarchies, physical and cultural barriers have been removed, and the couple come together simply as people in need of companionship – a final Carnivalesque image and accolade. This is repeated for higher stakes in the closing moments of *Brides, Bombs and Boardrooms* when the young Afghani feminist wheels the disabled antagonist Walter into the town square prior to his attempt to detonate an incendiary bomb. And a similar reversal is worked to comic and broadly anodyne effect in *Fete* when the fortune-teller applies her black Tarot spell on the festival proceedings to become, effectively, Carnival queen, presuming to govern subsequent proceedings in various ways: a local dignitary is injured; a distinguished service medal is mysteriously lost; the children seem to have disappeared. The Bakhtinian element in these various events is that festivals intended to reinforce the cultural hegemony have been subverted to turn the hegemony inside out. The town-twinning ceremony has been transformed into a private relationship between individuals who do not believe in the hegemony. The bomb attempt in a New Town centre is clearly intended to destroy the hegemony. And the comic subversion of the Church school fete replaces Christian orthodoxy with pagan ritual, after the orthodoxy has been exposed. The vicar has advised people, in certain circumstances, to steal, as he himself may have done. Instead of opening the fete, the vicar's wife lapses into a hysterical outburst in which she denounces her husband.

Games of chance are another key component of Bakhtin's Carnival:

> The images of the games were seen as a condensed formula of life and of the historic process: fortune and misfortune, gain and loss, crowning and uncrowning. Life was presented as a miniature play [...] *without footlights*.

(Rabelais and His World, p. 235)

This is immediately taken up at the beginning of *Strangers To Paradise* where the performers, enacting the parts of street vendors of everything from wares and services to lottery tickets and political causes, mingle with the crowd who are not entirely sure they are performers. Despite the announcement of the town-twinning ceremony, uncertainty persists as the performers erupt into various disputes arising from the transactions. The play ends at nightfall following another festival event in which the Polish fable of the Golden Duck features – a talisman of national import and the product of a deadly game of chance.

The machinations of the stock market – and the fortunes of the Regis family – represent the games of chance featured in *Brides, Bombs and Boardrooms*. The conduct of the games is not entirely legitimate, either on the part of the family or on the part of the banished son, banished ostensibly because he has married a Russian, but also guilty of faulty speculation on the futures market and, just recently, of a degree of malfeasance in using family stock as collateral for a flat, subverting the family's business dealings again. The climactic bombing, though a failure, is intended to blow up the town's shopping precinct, another of the family's enterprises. Inadvertently, the bomb, if detonated, would have killed Walter's wife, coerced into shady Russian speculation (a form of Russian roulette).

Games of chance figure most prominently in *Fete*, through the person of Kacey, the self-appointed soothsayer whose black artistry anticipates future events, including the crowning of the festival king and queen and the casting of various spells that render several of the characters deformed or at least physically impaired and finally the disappearance of the children.

The most important link between Bakhtin's Carnival and *Carnival Texts* is the grotesque body and its cultural ramifications. This may also be the most controversial aspect of *Carnival Texts* inasmuch as the author's view of Bakhtin and of his own work seems to be at odds with much of the prevailing wisdom about both.

There is a marked distinction between advancing a view for a socio-political cause and giving artistic expression to a subject. Bakhtin addresses this point as it relates to Carnivalesque reversal of roles:

> Crowning already contains the idea of immanent de-crowning: it is ambivalent from the very start. And he who is crowned is the antipode of a real king – a slave or a jester ... This ritual determine(s) a special de-crowning type of structure for artistic images and whole works, one in which the de-crowning (is) essentially ambivalent and two-levelled. If Carnivalistic ambivalence should happen to be extinguished ... they degenerat(e) into a purely negative exposé of a moral or socio-political sort, they become single-levelled, lose their artistic character and are transformed into naked journalism.

(Problems of Dostoevsky's Poetics, pp. 125–26)

This type of transformation is very near at hand in criticism that strives to be politically correct in examining work of a peculiarly sensitive nature – to do with race, gender or physical politics, for instance. Those who would favour advocacy over artistry in the depiction or analysis of physical deformity inevitably fall into the category of naked journalism. Bakhtin expressly states the ambivalent nature of Carnival by calling it two-levelled. Order is turned inside out, certainly, but not always to the same positive effect. He strikes a similar note of censure in *Rabelais and His World* when he takes issue with G Schneegan's view of the grotesque world of Rabelais:

> (He) ignores the deep ambivalence of the grotesque and sees it merely as a negation, an exaggeration pursuing narrowly satiric aims [...].

(Bakhtin and His World, p. 304)

Carnival Texts attempts an identical degree of ambivalence in its depiction of both authority reversal and the grotesque. This may be its greatest similarity to Bakhtin's Carnival. In the reversal effected by the Polish mayor's demand for war reparations in *Strangers To Paradise*, the aim is not simply or even essentially to satirize the vestiges of Imperial authority. Far more it is to use the elements of Carnival to facilitate the free play of cultural and physical diversity. The Polish mayor *claims* his forebears were prisoners of war. He offers no concrete evidence of this, nor is the demand followed by formal representation. He all but forgets the demand, in fact, in his subsequent dealings with the locals. What the demand does is to provide a Carnivalesque reversal that serves as a pretext for the removal of cultural barriers. Thereafter the East Europeans are shown to behave in an unrestrained way that exceeds British public decorum. Two women immediately erupt into a fist-fight that deviates even from British violence: it is vociferous without being fuelled by alcohol. A similar type of disorder is present in a scene where Polish sorters of refuse remonstrate against British sexual mores when they discover a used condom. Their verbal excess parallels the sexual excess they deplore, both expressing Carnivalesque licence.

The reversal in *Brides, Bombs and Boardrooms* depicts a Carnivalesque transference of power from a respectable British family to its disabled outcast. But this is not to say the outcast is beyond reproach. Even before attempting a terrorist act, he is guilty of malfeasance with regard to the flat. And in *Fete*, the deformed soothsayer exerts her demonic authority as a piece of vengeful blackmail against those who would rightfully exclude the woman's grossly miscreant daughter. Indeed, the woman exploits liberal sympathies towards her for deeply ambivalent aims of her own. The depiction of grotesque deformity in all three plays is intended to be ambivalent. For one thing, the grotesques are often bigoted (Bruno, Kiera and Pauline in *Strangers To Paradise*), unattractively manipulative (Walter in *Brides, Bombs and Boardrooms*, Kacey in *Fete*) or downright criminal (Bruno and Kacey).

Central to Bakhtin's conception of Carnival and the grotesque is the fundamentally populist belief that boundaries and hierarchies cease to exist during the festive occasion. This is the basis of the transformations of beggar to king and king to clown, not to satirize authority but to bring it within the orbit of everyday life. This, again, is related to Bakhtin's criticism of Schneegan's interpretation of Carnival: the aim is utopian, not satirical. The authority figure is stripped of authority in order to be at one with everyone else in the Carnival setting. This further explains the removal of barriers between audience and performer. Satire implies a difference in status as one group parodies the foibles of another. Carnival humour, on the other hand, posits laughter that is shared among the participants.

Bakhtin describes the origins of much medieval laughter as 'a victory over fear:'

All that is terrifying becomes grotesque … This grotesque image cannot be understood without appreciating the defeat of fear. The people play with terror and laugh at it; the awesome becomes a comic monster.

(*Rabelais and His World*, p. 91)

Carnival Texts takes this Carnivalesque notion of fear into laughter and applies it to twenty-first century attitudes towards physical deformity and, indeed, anything that is strange enough to evoke fear in the status quo. Bearing in mind that Carnival has already removed barriers of class and even of decorum, previous objects of fear now become sources of unbridled laughter, removed from the stigma of derision because they themselves promote the comedy. This is immediately evident in *Strangers To Paradise* when the play begins pre-ceremony with the routines of two of the physically deformed, Bruno Baglin and Kiera. They function in part as warm-up artists, priming the audience with routines designed to make them laugh or at least feel at ease. Bruno's is a shaggy-dog rant at the shoddy workmanship of East European builders. Racist in nature, as are many stand-up routines, it provokes laughter through its grotesque dimensions and character, delivered by a British grotesque. The source of the laughter is ambiguous: is it Bruno's blatant racism, or perhaps he is expressing thoughts a politically correct audience dare not utter? In any case, fear of the stranger – foreign and domestic – is dispelled.

Kiera's routine follows a similar pattern, even though it differs essentially in character as well as in intent. She is protesting against those who would harass her as a disabled person, getting her harassment in first, as it were. A lone protester with a placard announcing Harassment is Illegal, she strikes the audience immediately as a loon. They can see she is disabled, and perhaps they withhold outright condemnation because of it. But she does not evoke sympathy. Gradually, as they understand what she is doing, their distaste turns to amusement, particularly as her mother trails after her, apologizing, and the Polish-born Support Officer mistakes her for a Downs child in search of a seat near the front. Again, fear is transformed into laughter as both victim and potential perpetrator are reduced to comically grotesque objects. And the comedy is developed throughout the scene in the persons of the idiot-savant mayor and the two East European women squabbling beyond anyone else's comprehension. Other scenes of grotesque proportions follow, including the scene in the recycling plant and the fuss over the used condom–made even more comic by the final discovery of a dildo. British humour in such a circumstance might be based on badly concealed embarrassment. Here, the comedy is one of exaggeration. The woman reacts almost as though she has been raped. A final example of grotesque comedy in which fear is laughed away is a meeting between Kiera and the visiting mayor in her front garden when her fear is compounded by the realization that she may be related to him – much to her disgust – and she jokes that this may explain her physical deformity.

The conduct of both Walter (in *Brides*) and Kacey (in *Fete*) is altogether darker. But their proximity to the audience remains constant, as they, too, assume a pivotal place in the action. I take it as central to Bakhtin's concept of Carnival that the grotesque body is representative of the *vox populi*. So it was for me in the creation of these plays. Any actors choosing to work on this material have to adopt a relaxed attitude towards physical deformity, soon jettisoning any notions of political correctness that they might bring to the work. If grotesque realism is meant to challenge the status quo, as it surely does in Bakhtin's Carnival, then actors discovering these plays must also be prepared to abandon received wisdom. This is prerequisite to any discovery, and it is all the more evident with the physically grotesque.

Able-bodied performers undertaking roles as the physically deformed have been encouraged to disregard *disability* to concentrate on the human side of the characterization. Carnival's emphasis on excess and on exaggeration would seem to flout this advice to an alarming, almost retrograde, extent, and it would not surprise me if this approach drew criticism from the disability lobby, if only to say that twenty-first-century disability had moved beyond symbolic representation in art. But surely the one does not preclude the other. Something may have symbolic as well as actual resonance, as Bakhtin would be the first to argue for Carnival. My idea, anyway, was to create a world in which abnormality, increasingly, was the norm, especially with the distance between audience and performer diminishing before one's very eyes. Towards the end of *Strangers,* for example, the search is on for a specific disabled person, and a number of deformed characters appear. It is altogether desirable, in this context, if a number of oddly shaped members of the audience are under scrutiny, raising the vital questions, what constitutes deformity, what, exactly, is normality? No one, crucially, is being blamed for anything. So we might all qualify in a context where *everything* is permitted.

Audience reaction is virtually impossible to gauge. But in a context like this, where distinctions are blurred, any appreciation is as evident as it is welcome.

The ideal staging for a Carnivalesque performance is perhaps promenade, with audience members moving from scene to scene with the performers. These plays might all be performed as promenade spectacles, especially as they all conclude in a public square inviting group participation. They were written for ensemble performance, similar to a community play. As far as possible, the performers should remain in the space, perhaps assuming the guise of spectators when they are not performing. The plays, finally, were written for specific groups. But they lend themselves to free adaptation for a large number of performs. The only essential is the Carnival element whose principle, after all, is freedom and diversity.

Page references are to the 1984 English-language editions of each.

Note

1. Pages refer to 1984 English translation.

Works Cited

Problems of Dostoevsky's Poetics (trans. Caryl Emerson), Minneapolis: University of Minnesota Press, 1984.

Rabelais and His World (trans. Hélène Iswolsky), Bloomington: University of Indiana Press, 1984.

Problems of Dostoevsky's Poetics.

Bodies in Pain: Realism and the Subversion of Spectacle in *Brides, Bombs and Boardrooms*

John Lutz

'This isn't reality television – Minny Playfair, *Brides, Bombs and Boardrooms*

'Thus pain comes unsharably into our midst as at once that which cannot be denied and that which cannot be confirmed – Elaine Scarry, *The Body in Pain*

O pening with the narration of Minny Playfair, whose address to the audience explicitly denies that the play has anything in common with reality television or a party political broadcast, James MacDonald's *Brides, Bombs and Boardrooms* explores the difficulty of testifying to the reality of physical and psychic anguish in a culture where the sadistic enjoyment of pain has become a profitable enterprise. Harkening back to the chorus of ancient Greek drama, Minny Playfair's disclaimer plays a necessary role distinguishing this work from the kind of spectacle found on popular television, where pain has become a commodity that paradoxically anesthetizes the spectator to its felt reality. The subsequent drama, which she refers to as 'a public inquiry into an event that concerns us all,' aims to open up a space where suffering bodies can become visible. By referencing the spectacle of reality television, the opening narration sets up a dialogical relationship between itself and a dominant form of representing pain in contemporary popular culture in order to foreground the political, economic and cultural realities responsible for inflicting suffering on the disenfranchised. In some sense, the 'event' that Minny alludes to can be understood metaphorically as the forms of suffering rendered invisible by the dominant social and economic institutions of the western world. In a cultural context in which reality television makes use of the spectacle of other people's pain to minimize its reality, MacDonald, whose work frequently aims to expose the suffering of various marginalized groups by foregrounding their bodies, makes use of the conventions of spectacle in order to subvert the sadistic form that it occupies in the culture of reality television.

In her introduction to *The Body in Pain: The Making and Unmaking of the World*, Elaine Scarry characterizes the main subject of her book as an investigation into '[...] the difficulty of expressing physical pain [...] [and] the political and perceptual complications that arise as a result of that difficulty'(p. 3). This difficulty in expressing physical pain forms a consistent point of reference in *Brides, Bombs and Boardrooms*, where the interaction between the members of Walter's 'shameless middle-class household', Russian immigrants and criminals, and Muslim immigrants, establishes connections between ethnic discrimination, economic oppression and physical disability. As the one whose actions bring the remaining characters into each other's orbit, Walter is the central figure in the play, and his physical disability brings into focus the political issues that MacDonald aims to address. Indeed, physical disability plays a prominent role in many of MacDonald's comedies as a vehicle for addressing political and economic forms of oppression. As Thomas Fahy notes in his analysis of *Bread and Circus Freaks*, MacDonald '[...] offers a powerful critique of the social prejudices that limit, restrict, and interpret the disabled body' (Fahy 2002: 207) and indicts '[...] the systemic practices that attempt to render disability invisible' (Fahy 2002: 221). MacDonald's attention is not confined to disability, however, and his critique extends to other groups who experience disenfranchisement. As the director Martin Harvey notes, MacDonald's plays are 'peopled by outsiders, misfits, those who are often regarded as non-persons; the wrongly labelled who have to fight in order just to validate their existence' (Harvey 2008: 201). The description of MacDonald's characters as 'non-persons' provides an apt way to look at the connection between their invisibility and the invisibility of pain, since it calls attention to the manner in which the genuine recognition of the humanity of others requires the recognition of the reality of their suffering bodies. Unlike reality television, where the ideological boundaries reinforcing economic oppression and other forms of discrimination are reinforced and legitimated by the sadistic display of bodies in pain, *Brides, Bombs and Boardrooms* aims to explore the invisibility of physical pain from the standpoint of dominant middle-class values. This exploration includes the forms of physical and mental anguish visited upon those without economic security who are left vulnerable to the vicissitudes of the world capitalist market.

In effect, this requires giving a voice to physical pain in a way that makes it genuinely visible. The play's narrator/chorus announces this attention with a name, 'Playfair', that endorses her perspective as a 'fair' account of its subject while indicting middle-class culture for the way it promulgates 'unfair' representations of pain. These representations contribute to the reproduction of oppressive political and economic structures that transform many individuals into non-persons. In her investigation of the inexpressibility of physical pain, Scarry eloquently addresses the ways in which physical pain lacks a voice, but notes how in the process of finding a voice pain begins to tell a story. *Brides, Bombs and Boardrooms* represents an effort to give voice to pain. It tells a story about forms of suffering that frequently remain invisible to the dominant social and economic institutions of the western world. Indeed, in an interview with Thomas Fahy, MacDonald discusses how historically 'disabled people weren't widely visible in British society' (Fahy 2002: 112), and suggests that 'British society overall hasn't been good about dealing with *difference*. If it was, disability would be recognized, first of all, for what it is, and then dealt with humanely' (Fahy 2002: 112). As

MacDonald points out, both the issue of recognizing the reality of disability and the ability to deal with it humanely are inextricably intertwined; however, recognizing what disability 'is' requires a verbal objectification of suffering that testifies to its felt reality rather than the commodification of suffering found in the spectacle of reality television. *Brides, Bombs and Boardrooms* aims to produce a political representation of disability by exploring the reality of the kinds of pain endured by those who have been marginalized by the dominant representations of the mass media. This aim is limited not only by the misrepresentations of disability, but also by the difficulty in describing it. As Scarry points out in a discussion of the rights of the handicapped:

> ... if property (as well as the ways in which property can be jeopardized) were easier to describe than bodily disability (as well as the ways in which a disabled person can be jeopardized), then one would not be astonished to discover that a society had developed sophisticated procedures for protecting property rights long before it had succeeded in formulating the concept of 'the rights of the handicapped'. (1985: 12)

In order to endorse these rights, *Brides, Bombs and Boardrooms* must overcome two distinct but interrelated obstacles: the linguistic/artistic obstacle of verbally representing pain, and the political obstacle of shattering the middle-class misrepresentations that conceal it. Although disability provides the primary focus of the drama, the play's emphasis on suffering brings other marginalized and oppressed groups like displaced Russian and Muslim immigrants and women into the action in order to address the larger political and economic issues that put all of these groups in a shared position of vulnerability.

As such, it is not surprising that comedy is the main genre that MacDonald uses to disrupt the ideology of those institutions and open up spaces where, to borrow Scarry's language, 'the deep subterranean fact' or 'invisible geography' (1985: 3) of people's pain can be given a voice and embodied in a story. In *Brides, Bombs and Boardrooms*, one of the main vehicles for shattering middle-class assumptions is what Mikhail Bakhtin describes in *Rabelais and His World* as the carnival-grotesque. Bakhtin describes this comic form as a means

> ... to consecrate inventive freedom, to permit the combination of a variety of different elements and their rapprochment, to liberate from the prevailing point of view of the world, from conventions and established truths, from clichés, from all that is humdrum and universally accepted. (Bakhtin 1984: 34)

The conversation between Walter and his family at the beginning of the play places distinct cultural groups in dialogue with each other in a way that emphasizes the hierarchical organization of British society. It immediately begins to subvert class distinctions and open up a space for the political representation of the oppressed and marginalized by juxtaposing Walter's announcement to his family of his recent marriage to the Russian immigrant Lisa with Lisa's violent illness in a nearby bathroom. While Walter's family is clearly aware of

Lisa's suffering, their failure to acknowledge her pain is registered by their insensitivity and preoccupation with her economic motives for marrying Walter. In this scene, as in the rest of the play, individuals of differing rank who would otherwise never have had any genuinely intimate contact with each other are brought together in ways that call into question the legitimacy of the social hierarchy. As with all of the other characters in the play who identify themselves as respectable British citizens or pose as representatives of a just status quo, Walter's parents are subjected to a scathing satire for their inability to acknowledge the humanity of those who do not possess the proper social status or who depart from their normative assumptions.

Taking aim at the manner in which hierarchical thinking contributes to the inability to acknowledge the basic rights of others, the play consistently produces the kind of carnival atmosphere that Bakhtin viewed as a 'temporary liberation from the prevailing truth and from the established order' that enacts 'the suspension of all hierarchical rank, privileges, norms, and prohibitions' (Bakhtin 1984: 10). Furthermore, in his discussion of carnival in the Middle Ages, Bakhtin draws a distinction between carnival and the official feasts that represented the 'consecration of inequality' (Bakhtin 1984: 10). This distinction is also operative in *Brides, Bombs and Boardrooms* where the carnival-grotesque is made use of to disrupt conventional-middle class pieties rather than reinforce them. Unlike the 'official feasts' of reality television where middle-class values and social and economic inequality are reproduced in the sadistic display of pain, *Brides, Bombs and Boardrooms* points out the inhumanity of those who subscribe to a value system that perpetuates inequality and discrimination. In the process, the middle-class preoccupation with wealth, xenophobic attitude towards 'foreigners', and prejudices about physical disability are subjected to satire. When Walter informs his family about his new wife, conventional attitudes about disability and Russian immigrants as well as economic considerations form the basis of their response:

LOVEDAY: This was more than a first date.

PRUNELLA: No, unfortunately, I don't think it was. He met the girl, told her
             about us, offered us to her, and then [...] *she* told *him*. (*To WALTER*) Did
             she even bother to call you good looking?

LOVEDAY: He'll say she's too honest for that.

PRUNELLA: Naturally. 'I couldn't possibly want you for anything else. Please
             open accounts in my name'.

The smug cynicism exhibited by Prunella and Loveday suggests the limitations of the middle-class imagination and the narrowness of their vision. From their point of view, his disability makes it impossible that he could have been desired; consequently, Lisa must have married him for an underlying economic motive. The fact that she is Russian, and, as Loveday puts it, from 'Thieves' Paradise', reinforces their conviction that she is only after Walter's money. In addition, the marriage concerns them mainly because it affects the reputation of the family:

WALTER: All right, kick me out of the business.

PRUNELLA: We can't do that. You're my son, we're a reputable family, and your condition is potentially scandalous. We'd never hear the end of it.

Sound of toilet flushing.

Sounds like she's coming up for air.

Although Prunella pays lip service to her maternal obligation to Walter, her more powerful motives are clearly her concern with avoiding scandal. At the same time, the offstage sounds of Lisa violently vomiting provide an element of grotesque realism that emphasizes the extent to which Walter's family is incapable of recognizing either his humanity or the humanity of his Russian wife. Although Lisa's suffering is evident in the sounds that accompany her vomiting, her pain remains invisible to them because of their ideological investment in a social and economic hierarchy where the lives of foreigners are insignificant.

While the family's suspicion of Lisa is partly derived from an investment in a social hierarchy, they also respond to Walter's marriage to Lisa as an economic threat to their assets. When Walter's brother-in-law Stewart arrives with the news that the family business is threatened with a hostile takeover bid, Prunella suggests that Lisa might be behind it:

STEWART: I don't get this. What's going on? Walter's gone and got himself married?

LOVEDAY: To a Russian, no less.

PRUNELLA: Do you think she could be behind the takeover bid?

WALTER: She has no money! And why are you talking in front of her?

STEWART: You didn't go and give them a wedding present, did you?

LOVEDAY: We don't exactly approve of the match.

PRUNELLA: We didn't exactly know about it. That's the point. Walter disappears on a holiday weekend. When he comes back, I have a daughter-in-law! Wouldn't you expect me to be a little irate? (*To LISA*) No matter who it was?

On one level, Prunella's paranoid suspicion that Lisa might be behind the hostile takeover bid is absurd; however, her statement points out the connection between the xenophobic rejection of 'foreigners' and the ruthless methods that defend class privilege. Since Prunella views Lisa's marriage to Walter as an attempt to gain economic advantage, she places the hostile takeover bid of the family company in the same category. However, the primary satiric target of the passage is not Prunella, but the competitive class system of capitalism that reduces all human interaction to economic calculations of monetary loss or gain. Walter's family is utterly lacking in any of the bonds of sympathetic connection that one would expect in a genuine family, and their lack of compassion is directly linked to their mentally and emotionally impoverished focus on economic considerations. Indeed, this middle-class family can be viewed as representative not only of the British class system but also of the economic structure of global capitalism, a system in which, as Marx once eloquently phrased it, all human relations are reduced to the 'cash nexus'. The family's xenophobic reaction to Lisa is best understood within the framework of class conflict and economic competition. Lisa's marriage to Walter represents a 'hostile takeover bid' to Walter's family just as immigrants of all kinds appear to the British middle class (and the middle class of other western societies) as threats to their economic privilege. Their lack of sympathy for Lisa's suffering is emblematic of the systematic exclusion and denigration of anyone who can be scapegoated as a threat to middle-class economic prosperity.

Since Walter's family views all relationships primarily through the lens of economic considerations, it is not surprising that they are willing to sacrifice his health and well-being to preserve their company. His effort to gain economic support from a government agency, along with Lisa's attempt to extend her visa, not only provides an indictment of Walter's family, but also represents a satire directed at the ineffectual bureaucracy of the social institutions set up to care for the economically disadvantaged. Establishing a very clear connection between the plight of the disabled and the condition of the immigrant, the exchange between the comic bureaucratic functionaries, Janis and Stephie, emphasizes the economic vulnerability of the disenfranchised. The absurd obstacles that Walter and Lisa face in their attempts to secure assistance call attention to the moral bankruptcy of the institutions organized to help those rendered vulnerable to suffering:

JANIS: (*To WALTER*) And you'll have to go down to council HQ. We're not your convenience, you know. You told us severely disabled.

WALTER: I'm disabled. Look. (*He demonstrates*)

JANIS: That's genuine, is it? We're on the lookout for benefit cheats.

WALTER: I've nothing to hide. I've nothing, full stop. Ask my missus.

JANIS: [...] who just happens to be an illegal alien.

LISA: I am not illegal.

STEPHIE: But you say you've exceeded your visitor's visa. (*Interrupts her protest*) There's no desperate rush. They're not going to escort you out in the morning. The worst they could do is place you in a detention centre, but you're a lone woman, so it's not likely.

LISA: Ah-ha. Like a prison, you mean.

While exposing the brutality of social services and the forms of degradation experienced by those who lack social and economic status, the exchange above illustrates how additional suffering is inflicted upon those who are already in pain. In an absurd minimalist duet that sometimes evokes Beckett's comic doubling, Janis and Stephie provide the focus of MacDonald's satirical exploration of the lack of rights for the disabled, immigrants and the disadvantaged. Although both Walter and Lisa are genuinely in need, Janis and Stephie treat them in a way that stigmatizes them for their conditions. Walter is accused of being a benefit cheat and Lisa is characterized as an 'illegal alien' in a way that criminalizes them. Lisa's insight that the detention centre is a prison reinforces the connection between the criminalization of the poor, the disabled and immigrants in order to place it in the context of British society's ruthless defense of middle-class interests. The criminalization of the poor, the disabled and immigrants renders them responsible for their own suffering in a way that absolves the middle-class observer of any moral responsibility or complicity in their oppression.

Throughout the scene with Janis and Stephie, the stigmatizing of Walter and Lisa continues in a way that calls attention to a series of binary oppositions driving the middle-class perspective and legitimizing its privileges. When Janis learns that Walter has lost his position as company director and had his assets frozen, she attempts to stigmatize him as a white collar criminal in a passage that aims to expose a series of oppositions implicit in the middle-class value system:

JANIS: Why? Are you a white collar criminal? They discovered you cooking the books?

LISA: Who is criminal, Walter? His own mother kick him out!

JANIS: I don't understand – it's a family firm? You've been a naughty boy?

LISA: Naughty, yes. He marry with me. Dirty Russian.

JANIS: You're not serious

WALTER: My family believe in 'fortress Britain,' you see, and a lady from the Evil Empire, well, she's worse than Scheherazade.

JANIS: But they ought to be grateful. I mean in your condition…well, it's not to everyone's taste, if you'll pardon my bluntness.

WALTER: Not at all. They felt exactly the same.

Beginning with the distinction between criminal and non-criminal, a number of binary pairs emerge in this passage, including dirty/clean, naughty/nice, non-citizen/citizen, disabled/non-disabled and non-European/European. A few lines after the passage above the European Union emerges as yet another category. Each of these binary pairs is presented in order to address the unspoken assumption of the middle-class value system that only clean, nice, non-disabled, non-criminal, European citizens are entitled to the full measure of their humanity. As Walter and Lisa's experiences with Janis and Stephie are intended to indicate, all others need not apply. Indeed, the satiric thrust of the scene is intended to expose the ideological mechanisms responsible for determining who counts and who does not. The overarching binary pair that encompasses all of the others presented in the play is the category of non-human/human. Interestingly, it is Lisa's response to Janis's suggestion that Walter is a criminal that challenges the binary thinking that legitimates his family's actions: she expresses outrage at Janis's question by suggesting that Prunella's act of kicking out her own son is the real crime.

When Walter suffers a mild stroke in response to the frustration and stress created by his inability to succour economic aid, the human body in pain is once again placed in the foreground. After his seizure, the satire directed at the middle class takes on an increasingly harsh dimension as Minny Playfair initiates a dialogue with the audience designed to ironically subvert the self-satisfied platitudes subscribed to by respectable British citizens:

MINNY: What would *you* do in this situation – treat him privately, sending the bill to his family? I fancy even the most hard-hearted among us would sooner collapse ourselves than do nothing for Walter. Face it, we're hopelessly soft in many ways […] when you think about other countries. Walter was rushed to the hospital after suffering what was assessed as a mild stroke, his personal circumstances put to one side. We still treat the patient, not his bank balance.

Minny's direct address of the audience implicates them in the drama and is intended to point out their complicity in the forms of inhumanity represented throughout the play. Her suggestion that many in the audience would have enough sympathy for Walter to help him represents a satiric indictment of their inaction and moral complacency in response to human suffering. Immediately following the grotesque spectacle of Walter's contorted body having a seizure, Minny's interrogation of the conscience of the audience dramatically points out how British institutions do nothing for the disabled, immigrants and the poor because they are considered non-persons. Her commentary about the softness of Britain compared to other countries and about treating the patient rather than his bank balance ironically subverts the standard rationalizations used to defend middle-class privilege and justify the brutality of the system. The satiric treatment of these rationalizations makes a powerful statement about the harshness of British society and emphasizes the extent to which a person's worth is clearly connected to his or her monetary value.

Moving forward three days to an account of Walter's experience in the hospital, Minny's narration describes how Walter is being cared for by Jameela, a political refugee from Afghanistan fleeing oppression by the Taliban who experiences post-September 11 discrimination against Muslims in Britain. Minny's ironic subversion of middle-class values continues as she relates Walter's experiences in sotto voce intended to create a sarcastic tone:

> [...] (sotto voce): It's been three days now, and they're on the point of releasing him. But there are two things worth noting here. I wonder how many can spot them [...] All right, where exactly are they going from here and who are the people in charge of the case? They're not British, are they.

JAMEELA: You don't have to rub it in.

MINNY: But isn't that very much the point?

JAMEELA: If they didn't need us, they wouldn't employ us. Or do you think it's easy to dodge people's prejudices the whole time. You're British, so how can you know?

While continuing to subvert class distinctions and the hierarchical organization of British society by bringing another cultural group into the action, this scene emphasizes the connection between the binary thinking that grants outsiders subhuman status and the exploitation of labour. Not only does British society fail to provide care for many of their own, but also it fails to recognize the degree to which the labour of many of those who are discriminated against contributes to its prosperity. In the depiction of a Muslim woman caring for a disabled, penniless British citizen, MacDonald calls attention to the moral bankruptcy of the middle-class value system that supports an economy in which those who perform the labour of caring are abused and denigrated. In the exchange between Walter and Jameela, the prejudices of the British middle class are continually subjected to criticism as Walter undergoes a comic conversion to Islam that underscores the importance of recognizing the pain of others and the inhumanity of a system devoid of compassion.

Jameela's care of Walter, along with her willingness to take him into her home, puts a spotlight on the systematic discrimination that enables exploited labourers like Jameela to be viewed as interlopers stealing British jobs:

JAMEELA: Don't worry Walter. We'll look after you.

WALTER: (*Near tears of rage*) What are *you* still doing here?

JAMEELA: You mean taking your best British jobs?

WALTER: I mean in this tight-arsed fuck-of-a-country!

JAMEELA'S home. She and WALTER are going through his regular exercises. WALTER'S face has a twisted expression.

MINNY: It may come as a shock to many of you just how many have come from abroad [...] I mean qualified people like Walter's pair [...] head-hunted. And they include, of course, doctors from Afghanistan. And if we depend on them, can we really object to their presence? It's a bit like cheering your home side, filled with African players, and then saying they're not entitled to the best that this country has to offer. We certainly don't stack up very well against these people. They've given Walter – a total stranger – the run of their home. He's claimed it, almost as his territorial right.

While taking satirical aim at the xenophobic, middle-class fear of foreigners taking professional jobs, Minny Playfair lives up to her name by exposing the injustice of a system that denigrates those who perform needed and useful work. Her analogy of cheering for a home team comprised of players who are denied the rights enjoyed by those doing the cheering points out the moral contradiction of depending upon immigrants to do the labour and then excluding them from the advantages of full citizenship. Furthermore, the analogy also points out the exploitative nature of the relationship between privileged British citizens, who are spectators observing the labour performed, and underprivileged citizens and non-citizens alike, who do the work, but gain no benefits besides surviving to work another day. Even Walter is not completely immune to the ideology supporting class privilege since he claims Jameela's home as if it were his 'territorial right,' an allusion to the British occupation of Afghanistan in the nineteenth and twentieth centuries that underscores the historical role of imperialism in contemporary British prosperity. By pointing out the economic and social forms of injustice inflicted upon those who inhabit the negative side of the various binary oppositions subsumed under the category of human/inhuman, the play inverts this opposition so that the respectable middle class and the institutions of British society are exposed for their inhumanity.

However, even with the vast array of outsiders presented up until this point in the play, MacDonald is not finished with smashing cherished middle-class beliefs and shattering conventional pieties. Preparing the ground for the denouement of the play, the experiences of Jameela her husband, Hamid, and her sister-in law, Farida as targets of racist violence and police surveillance and arbitrary arrest in the post-September 11 era shed light on how British institutions inflict gratuitous pain on those who are already vulnerable and suffering. At one point, Hamid describes the asylum process for Muslim refugees as 'torture' and references Guantanamo Bay when explaining the pain that his family has endured as a consequence of being misidentified as terrorists. These references suggest the way that the binary opposition between non-terrorist and terrorist has been assimilated to the other oppositions in operating in British society. When Walter turns out to be the one who planted the bomb at the end of the play, this opposition is also questioned. Even though Walter's role as a terrorist functions as a comic absurdity in the play, it exposes how binary thinking works to exclude immigrants, the poor and the disabled from the privileges of so-called normal, respectable citizens. Walter's explanation for his act establishes it as a blow against all forms of exclusion:

WALTER: Why not? You don't think my efforts are worth it, is that it? The cripple's worth only a caution because he missed?

MINNY: This is one time that you can be thankful for your condition.

WALTER: Are you sure about that? This isn't the Special Olympics of Terrorism. You can't sort us like you'd sort out the under-fives. Several lifetimes have gone into this. Several civilizations. Let me beg you all to be ready for it, because some time, sooner than you know, we're not going to miss. You should have killed us when you had the chance.

Pin spot on WALTER.

According to the logic of the opposition between human and non-human that encompasses all of the other binaries in the play, the most vulnerable individuals in the world, those who suffer the most, are the enemies of society. *Brides, Bombs and Boardrooms* aims to point out the absurdity of binary reasoning by foregrounding the pain of those who are denied their basic human rights as a result of being neatly placed into a negative category. By parodying the horrific spectacle of terrorism at the end of the play, MacDonald evokes the reality of bodies in pain and subverts the sadistic spectacle of suffering on reality television where the non-human status of outsiders is reinforced. Walter's last sentence speaks not only for the disabled, but for all outsiders whose suffering is rendered invisible by discrimination. The incongruous image of the disabled terrorist deconstructs the various binary oppositions presented in the play and aims to dramatically call attention to real bodies in pain. The image aims to transcend the ideological limitations that prevent the suffering of the disenfranchised from being acknowledged or their stories from being heard.

Works Cited

Bakhtin, Mikhail (1984), *Rabelais and His World*, Bloomington: Indiana University Press.

Fahy, Thomas (2002), 'An Interview with James MacDonald', in Thomas Fahy and Kimball King (eds), *Peering Behind the Curtain: Disability, Illness, and the Extraordinary Body in Contemporary Theater*. New York: Routledge, pp. 111–115.

Fahy, Thomas (2008), 'Freaks, Food, and Fairy Tales: Confronting the Limits of Disability in *Bread and Circus Freaks*', in James MacDonald (ed), *Russia, Freaks, and Foreigners: Three Performance Texts*, Bristol: Intellect, 207–215.

Harvey, Martin (2008), 'Director's Notes', in James MacDonald (ed), *Russia, Freaks, and Foreigners: Three Performance Texts* Bristol: Intellect, pp. 201–206.

Scarry, Elaine (1985), *The Body in Pain: The Making and Unmaking of the World*, New York: Oxford University Press.

Blowing Up the Nation: Vulnerability and Violence in James MacDonald's Post-national England

Jessica O'Hara

James MacDonald's *Brides, Bombs and Boardrooms* depicts contemporary England as a mixing bowl of disaffection and anxiety where nobody really blends in or belongs. Minny Playfair, the compère of the play, promises the audience that the action about to unfold is not reality television . However, her role as hostess of this action rife with hostility, backstabbing, paranoia, vulnerability and competition certainly mimics the conventions of the television genre she disavows. Though comedic and even farcical at times, the play rigorously examines the bad reality show of Britain caught up in a siege mentality against its most recent wave of immigrants from Eastern Europe, Afghanistan and Africa. While *Brides, Bombs and Boardrooms* has much in common with the work of Salman Rushdie and Caryl Churchill in exploring the marginal and hybrid positions of the immigrant, postcolonial and gendered subject in imperial and post-imperial contexts, MacDonald's work represents the next generation of writing on these themes. For many writers of the previous generation, England, Englishness and Empire still function as referents and historical frameworks for understanding citizenship and identity. In MacDonald's work, these referents pretty much disappear. Englishness is less a guarantee of character or citizenship than a kind of talisman that works only intermittently. Indeed, while the immigrants of the piece are surely vulnerable to the vicissitudes of fortune – and immigration policy – this vulnerability extends to the native English as well, where no birthright is too secure, no affiliation too stable or no fortune too protected. England itself hardly seems to exist as a nation or a homeland: a real, rooted place. Rather, in the play, the concept of the nation as a set of principles, places and traditions is reduced to a mishmash of laws, inaccessible entitlement programmers, overlapping bureaucracy, EU policies and policing tactics – all favoring nobody. Even the play's setting, which is designated as Middle England, gives way to a newly constructed, faux town centre, a vaguely European nowhere, in the play's final scene.

In many ways, MacDonald's work, with its wicked playfulness and irony, recalls that of his fellow playwright and collaborator Caryl Churchill, who, thirty years earlier, wrote

Cloud Nine, a landmark Joint Stock Theatre Group play that probed the relationships among imperialism, gender and identity. Act One of *Cloud Nine* is set in Victorian-era colonial Africa, while Act Two is set in London in 1979, one hundred years later. For the characters in the play, however, only 25 years have passed. In her notes on *Cloud Nine*, Churchill explains why she compressed the play's historical timeline: When the company talked about their childhoods and the attitudes to sex and marriage that they had been given when they were young, everyone felt that they had received very conventional, almost Victorian expectations and that they had made great changes in their lifetimes (p. 246). For Churchill, the legacies of high British colonialism in structuring identities extend far beyond the Empire's historical reality; thus, in Act Two of *Cloud Nine*, the characters seek to wrest their identities from the rigid binaries of Empire, which Churchill's play exposes as pernicious and false in Act One through a series of comically perverse and hypocritical relations. In Act Two, the Empire recedes as a lived reality and ideological construct, though it still lingers in the distance as the characters map out new sexual and political identities. Things are messy, and there are still residual problems from Empire, such as when one character's brother, a British soldier, is killed in Northern Ireland. However, despite these colonial hangovers, there is a sense of reconciliation and tentative progress. While *Cloud Nine* postulates that Englishness was founded on imperial and patriarchal domination, which the play's action exposes and condemns, the last line sounds a surprising note of sympathy, as Clive, the play's arch- imperialist and patriarch, waxes nostalgic: I used to be proud to be British. There was a high ideal. I came out on the verandah and looked at the stars (p. 320).

In *Brides, Bombs and Boardrooms*, which shares *Cloud Nine*'s ironic reshuffling of characters and allegiances, there is no such high mindedness, albeit misguided or even deluded, about what it means to be English. Englishness itself, though frequently referenced in the play, seems to dissolve, as Lisa finds no solace – or citizenship – in marrying Walter, and the native English characters think of nothing beyond their own bank account and personal security. More so, the meditations about Englishness, postcolonial citizenship and migrant identities found in works by authors like Salman Rushdie seem to vaporize in MacDonald's hands, as England's contemporary immigration concerns are not the direct political legacy of the former British Empire, as the recent wave of eastern Europeans and Russians to Britain do not readily play into the post-imperial discourses of centre and periphery. Indeed, the play's encounter between a former colonizer and colonized subject does not directly involve Britain; it takes place when Lisa, a Russian from the former Soviet Union, meets Jameela, Walter's Afghan nurse, in the English hospital.

The vertiginous sense of complexity and chaos *Brides, Bombs and Boardrooms* invokes seems created by a failure in contemporary discourse to develop satisfying paradigms of affiliation and responsibility, or a failure to narrate the nation. Benedict Anderson and Earnest Gellner, both theorists of nationhood, posit that national affiliation is formulated through selective narration, a kind of patchwork of past events that are imbued with teleological significance. Postcolonial theorist Edward Said also examines the role of writing and narrative in colonial and cultural domination. He famously argues in his landmark 1979 book *Orientalism* that it is through Orientalist discourse, or various narratives about the East or the Other, that the West comes to know itself. Said defines Orientalism in part as a style of thought based upon an ontological and epistemological distinction made between 'the Orient' and [...] the Occident. Thus a very large mass of writers, among whom are poets, novelists, philosophers, political theorists, economists and imperial administrators, have accepted the basic distinction between East and West as the starting point (p. 21). Said tries to demonstrate that European culture gained strength and identity by setting itself off against the Orient as a sort of surrogate and even underground self (p. 22).

Though these narratives perform some violence to truth, as it were, they also offer a sense of purpose and identity to subjects, even in resisting such narratives. As we see in *Cloud Nine*, colonial Englishness is defined against the Other, but in the ebb of colonialism, new identities could be forged *against the Englishness* that was forged *against the 'Other'*. In many senses, then, postcolonial discourse still preserves the referent of the Empire, and an overarching narration, or meta-narrative, as postmodern theorist François Lyotard calls it, of the English nation (as *not that, not now*) can still be scripted. However, Lyotard points out that we postmodern subjects have become sceptical of meta-narratives – like narratives of nationhood – for their failure to accommodate heterogeneity and difference into their schema. Lyotard argues in *The Postmodern Condition: A Report on Knowledge* that postmodern narrative puts forward the unpresentable in presentation itself; that which denies itself the solace of good forms, the consensus of a taste that would make it possible to share collectively the nostalgia for the unattainable; that which searches for new presentations, not in order to enjoy them but in order to impart a stronger sense of the unpresentable (p. 81).

In *Brides, Bombs and Boardrooms*, the contrarities and heterogeneity of experience seem too vast and too ironic to be accommodated and shaped, and instead, Lyotard's micro-narratives – smaller, localized stories of affiliation (or, in the play's case, failed and disastrous affiliations – proliferate. In the play's emblematic final scene, most of the characters, who meet up in pairs or arrive upon the scene, are separated from one another in purpose and understanding and are feeling vulnerable or wronged. Indeed, several characters could have planted the bomb, and, in fact, a handful of them get arrested for it. Such is the state of play, as it were, in contemporary England, which seems a hotbed of fear, estrangement and betrayal where self-preservation, rather than a shared purpose and a sense of belonging, becomes the common thread.

While Lyotard prefers the micro-narrative to the meta-narrative of nationhood, MacDonald's work demonstrates that the absence of a national discourse on character, affiliation and assimilation inaugurates an uncomfortable era, a vacuum of responsibility and humanity. Especially in the past decade or so, scholars from across disciplines have been theorizing and studying what is often termed post-nationalism, the conditions of which are generally named as international capital investment, fluid national borders, supra-national possibilities for citizenship, the presence of global media culture, and the proliferation of multinational corporations. Such studies often consider that if the nation state no longer coheres and can no longer be narrativized, then perhaps new modalities of citizenship shall become our means of understanding responsibility and affiliation. However, *Brides Bombs, and Boardrooms* shows with much humour that such concepts of citizenship also fail. In the play, the rhetoric and realities surrounding citizenship are less about individual rights and modalities of belonging than about public burden, detection and exclusion. Lawyers, advocates and bureaucrats need to be called in to determine who is a legal citizen, a worthy asylum seeker or a charge of the state. The Byzantine, sometimes competing criteria seem designed to root out almost everybody, as the scene at the bed and breakfast with Janis and Steffie underscores:

STEPHIE: Anybody. I've cited you the best case I know for asylum, and that's due to go down the Sewanee, and yours is several degrees worse. Between hopeful and no hope, you're hovering somewhere round beside-the-point. And don't even contemplate slipping in between the cracks. *I* couldn't be party to that, but you'd never get away with it, as others have found to their cost.

WALTER: I haven't asked for that, have I?

STEPHIE: Like saying she has an executive job when she hasn't. They'll want avadavats … testimonials from her employers. You say you don't work?

WALTER: My family made that impossible […] because of Lisa.

STEPHIE: *(after a beat)* We'll draft a letter to say you're an […] invalid. Your GP will write in support. You need your wife here to look after you, how's that?

JANIS: And I'm sure she could claim care allowance.

STEPHIE: Good God, don't do that […] at least until we've submitted something.

JANIS: Well, they don't have to own up to everything, do they? I'm for everyone claiming as much as they can, to be frank with you. I took this when my Morris injured himself in a road accident […] and you'd think we're entitled to everything going. The rival insurers with their no-claims crooks (excuse me) ended up proving it was our fault. Morris was driving without due care and attention. And now he can barely walk. He has whatever they'll give him, and no, he's not playing golf or making charity walks on the side. I wanted children, and now I've got him. *(To LISA)* You claim what you can, love, with our blessing. I'm here to help anyone who's entitled.

STEPHIE: I don't think there's much more to be done for the moment.

JANIS: I shouldn't be very much longer, myself [...] It too is on a point system, but I'll give this the highest recommendation, call it urgent, well, yes, it's a B and B.

This exchange and many others like it in the play unfailingly cast its characters as victims of the system such that qualifications are under- or over-shot or compromised by any number of mitigating factors. Even needing aid, asserting rights or assisting others can call down unwanted attention and vulnerability, even from voodoo curses, as Gina, the proprietor of the B and B, imagines!

If English citizenship seems an impoverished way to foster notions of belonging and affiliation, supra-national or global citizenship is even worse in MacDonald's text. Indeed, EU membership and UN asylum policies hardly guarantee a warm welcome in a host country, but instead function as a neat card trick:

STEPHIE: They operate on a point system now. So many points gains admission. Fifty points for a Ph.D. [...] skills the qualified national lacks. *(Beat)* You're not getting this, are you. If you had a job in a bank, say, with connections to the new Russia [...]

LISA: I hate the new Russia. *(Fakes spitting)* Phoo, *blin*. I want away.

STEPHIE: I was afraid of that. You're not French, are you, coming from Paris? If you lived there, maybe you're part of the Union.

LISA: I never want to hear part-of-union again. I married to British.

STEPHIE: That no longer counts, with all the new immigrants from the Union [...]

LISA: Ahh!

If there already exists a depleted sense of national affiliation, then regional connection, as the European Union promises, is even more contrived and forced, a political and commercial entity rather than a lived identity.

While citizenship seems a fraught, if not bankrupt, notion, cleaving to one's own people is a downright dangerous move. After marrying English fails Lisa, she is impelled to follow her mother and put herself in the care of her own countrymen, which entangles her in a web of obligation and threat outside of the official immigration channels. Farida is similarly burdened by her relations' Soviet connections. She rebels against Hamid's entreaties to adopt a westernized identity and mocks his mimicry of English dress and ways. While Lisa wants to disavow the new Russia, Farida wants to embrace her fundamentalist Islamic identity, and neither desire seems particularly viable.

The Islamic faith offers the only vestigial remains of community and responsibility in the play (which is ironic, given that it is associated with a supra-national organization that is far from peace loving: Al Qaeda). Indeed, Jameela, Hamid and Farida take Walter in because, as Farida explains, 'The Quran bids us to help the enfeebled'. Their care of Walter is the one instance of charity and humanity in the whole play. And, as Minny Playfair observes:

It may come as a shock to many of you just how many have come from abroad […] I mean qualified people like Walter's pair … head-hunted. And they include, of course, doctors from Afghanistan. And if we depend on them, can we really object to their presence? It's a bit like cheering your home side, filled with African players, and then saying they're not entitled to the best that this country has to offer. We certainly don't stack up very well against these people. They've given Walter – a total stranger – the run of their home. He's claimed it, almost as his territorial right.

The irony Minny points out is that immigrants who are often assumed to be seeking asylum were recruited to aid the *British* population. In Walter's case, he literally finds asylum in them. While the piety and virtue of religion, one of the oldest institutions and meta-narratives, seems to offer a paradigm of responsibility and protection for the vulnerable, it can also lead to violence. Walter, a new convert to Islam, channels his bitterness and helplessness into its teachings and understands the religion as a vehicle for punishment and revenge. Rather than bringing him closer to others, his Islamic faith alienates him further from his Aunt Henny and makes reconciliation with his family and Lisa impossible. It is also ironic that the bombing at the end of the play – an act of Islamic terrorism, if that is what it can be termed – comes at the hands of a disabled native-born Briton who owns the very thing he blows up to punish the infidels, his very own people. Much of the discourse surrounding radical Islam suggests that it preys upon those with no hope, so it is yet again an ironic twist that someone like Walter, who, aside from his disability, was born into a life of western privilege, could become so disaffected and marginalized.

While *Brides, Bombs and Boardrooms* highlights the very instability of identity and relationships in contemporary Britain, it also foregrounds the shifting terrain of the homeland. Though the Regis family seems to represent English wealth and interests in this play, it is curious that MacDonald does not cast them as *landed* gentry or even captains of industry. Their home is, as Minny Playfair describes it, shamelessly middle class rather than a Mayfair townhouse or country estate . MacDonald's characterization of the Regis family thus strays from the clichéd parable of the foreign-born invader making her way into the hallowed inner sanctum of British life. The Regis family are not the Windsors, though their surname bespeaks royalty; they have not held ancestral estates and family fortunes for centuries, and their wealth seems utterly tentative. Indeed, it seems as if the Regis family does not really own much but stocks and liquid assets, and as such, their wealth is intangible, illusory and incredibly vulnerable, as this charged family scene indicates:

STEWART: You're all here – great. Walter, this concerns you, too. Pay attention. *(Looks at LISA but does not really acknowledge her)* There's been a serious hostile bid.

PRUNELLA: What did I tell you? *(To STEWART)* Get onto Joshua Markby. He'll know exactly what needs to be done.

LOVEDAY: Stewart's in charge now, Mater. You say serious – how so?

STEWART: Well, they got hold of the quarterly trade figures, saw our shares plummet, purchased a huge volume of bonds from the bank … we had to expect it, really.

PRUNELLA: Who is it, British company?

LOVEDAY: Oh, it wouldn't matter if they were, ultimately, Japanese. *(To STEWART)* Who do you have in mind for the rival bid?

STEWART: No one. You don't want control out of the family, do you. We're going to issue a load of dual-credit stock […] *(To PRUNELLA)* Shares that are worth less than yours so they can't get a seat on the board. Even with only 4 per cent stock, you'd still own 52 per cent of the company. We need, though, to buy Walter out.

PRUNELLA: I don't understand. We own much more than four percent, Stewart. What are you talking about?

STEWART: Oh, God, yes. I'm saying if. Hypothetically, on paper. If your stock options amounted to only a total of four percent, you'd still have control, because they're worth more than everyone else's.

This almost nonsensical boardroom cant draws attention to the quixotic nature of international financial markets in a climate where economic meltdowns and business scandals are by-words. Wealth is ephemeral, ungrounded and unreal on this contemporary business stage.

Just as wealth is fleeting and intangible, the land itself seems to be losing its sense of place, unmooring itself from history and specificity. Significantly, the play's action culminates in a brand new town centre, a mere simulation of community and quaintness. Minny describes the setting:

We're festively met in a burgeoning shopping precinct in one of the new towns like Telford or Milton Keynes, though it's probably closer to London than that. There are restaurants and pavement cafes and haute couture shops with more staff than clientele in them. They'll close down once the first quarter's sales come due, and then this whole area will begin to look like a giant squat. But right now it's a harbinger of hope, an oasis in the desert of downturn.

These new spaces are fascinating because they long for the atmosphere of comfort and belonging evoked by a European street scene, yet they are mere contrivances of that timeless, rooted intimacy. Indeed, their very existence signals contemporary culture's conspicuous consumerism and preference for simulated experience, a symptom of the postmodern condition, as theorist Jean Baudrillard contends. It seems significant, then, that the characters would converge upon this a-historical, simulated nowhere, a faux public square that Walter's family somehow owns, a place that has no connection to any character in the play. Just as the characters fail to connect to one another, they also fail to connect to the space in which they live. Is it any wonder that someone tries to blow it up?

Brides, Bombs and Boardrooms catches its characters in a historical moment that knows not what it is, when traditional guiding principles, such as nationhood, citizenship, religion and fair play, have lost their force, and where no proper paradigm for affiliation, responsibility or even humanity has yet emerged. Indeed, even the family, the most intimate and basic unit of affiliation, seems to have dissolved in this environment of vigorous self-preservation. Moreover, post-national England seems unable to decide whether it is too cruel or not cruel enough. At the play's end, after Tamara suggests that Walter would not be tortured by the police because of his condition, Walter rejoins, 'Are you sure about that?' This isn't the Special Olympics of Terrorism. You can't sort us like you'd sort out the under-fives. Several lifetimes have gone into this. Several civilizations. Let me beg you all to be ready for it, because some time, sooner than you know, we're not going to miss. You should have killed us when you had the chance. Walter's unclear referent for us (is he referring to the disabled? Muslim extremists? The generally disaffected? Everybody?) hints at the idea that the contemporary age is standing on the precipice of some violent change, one that we – everyone who is to blame and everyone who is vulnerable (and everyone seems to be in both categories) – all have coming. As such, the play presents contemporary Britain as a powder keg of tension that literally is about to blow.

Works Cited

Churchill, Caryl (1978), *Plays: One*, London: Methuen.

Lyotard, François (1979), *The Postmodern Condition: A Report on Knowledge* (trans. eoff Bennington and Brian Massumi), Minneapolis: University of Minnesota Press.

Said, Edward (1996), 'From *Orientalism*' in Padmini Mongia (ed), *Contemporary Postcolonial Theory: A Reader*, New York: Arnold Press, pp. 20–36.

Notes on Contributors

James MacDonald has written many plays over nearly half a century, staged in London, Edinburgh and south-western England. He has also written a major essay on disability, *The Virtue of Living a Lie*, published in Britain and in the United States.

John Lutz is an assistant professor of English at Long Island University, C.W. Post Campus. He received a Ph.D. in Comparative Literature (1998) from The State University of New York at Stony Brook and an M.A. (1991) and B.A. (1989) in English Literature from Long Island University. He teaches philosophy and literature, postcolonial literature and theory, political philosophy, and twentieth-century literature. His most recent publications include articles in *Conradiana, Texas Studies in Literature and Language, LIT*, and *Research in African Literatures, Rethinking Marxism*, and *Mosaic*.

Jessica O'Hara earned her Ph.D. in English from The University of North Carolina-Chapel Hill. Her dissertation, *Undercover Irishness: Espionage, Empire, and Identity in Irish Literature, 1880–2000*, examines literary representations of Irish ambivalence and unreliability in the imperial matrix. She is currently a lecturer in English at Penn State University, where she teaches English composition, literary theory, and British, Irish and postcolonial literature courses. Her current work continues her focus on national identity and migrant culture in contemporary British and Irish contexts.

Thomas Fahy (essay coordinator) is an associate professor of English and Director of the American Studies Program at Long Island University, C. W. Post. He has published eleven books, including *Freak Shows and the Modern American Imagination* (2006); *Gabriel García Márquez's Love in the Time of Cholera: A Reader's Guide* (2003); three horror novels, *Sleepless* (2009), *The Unspoken* (2008) and *Night Visions* (2004); and several edited collections – *The Philosophy of Horror* (2010), *Considering David Chase* (2007), *Considering Alan Ball* (2006), *Considering Aaron Sorkin* (2005), *Captive Audience: Prison and Captivity in Contemporary Theater* (2003) and *Peering Behind the Curtain: Disability, Illness, and the Extraordinary Body in Contemporary Theater* (2002).